REVIEWS

First off, Hamburger says that his friend Mark saw an actual ninja, but that's bullshit, because there are less than fifty ninjas in the whole world and there are even less than that in the U.S. Second, I've been inside a real *Okinawan* dojo (I bet Hamburger doesn't even know what that is) and I know what I'm talking about. Maybe when Hamburger turns eleven, he can ask his mommy if she'll get him a life for his birthday.

—T.B. Lawson, age 33

This book changed my life. When I grow up, I want to kill someone!

—Cindy, age 7½

I am a single mother. A single mother of three boys! And it's tough enough to keep them from acting up without people like Robert Hamburger in the world. He is a disgrace to the whites, if he's white. My second-born son has been, as he calls it, "flipping out" recently and he started doing so around the same time the boys discovered this book. And surprise, surprise, my son seriously harmed his brother AND now his behavior is affecting his schoolwork. Is Robert Hamburger going to tutor him? Doubt it. I'm a single mother! My son's rambunctious attitude is going to get him put in juvenile hall or even jail. Hamburger is encouraging kids to go berserk and disregard rules. I demand that this book be banned, before someone seriously gets hurt. Trust me, Mr. Hamburger, this is one single mother of three boys you do not want to mess with. I'll see you in court! Write me back and we'll talk some more.

—a-single-mother-of-three-boys-you-do-not-want-to-mess-with, age 41

I use the martial arts (no, not ninjitsu . . . I don't have the patience or dedication) in conjunction with medieval sword skills. So I have a working knowledge of <u>what it takes</u> to become proficient in ANY form of the martial arts, even the complicated ones. There is a reason why Ninjitsu is called an ART. Figure that part out, Hamburger. . . . Oh, wait. . . . Sorry. . . . He probably doesn't have enough grey matter (brain) for that. Hamburger is the opposite of what any human being should even think of being. He thinks he knows everything (but actually, he knows nothing). Other people know that he's full of crap, too. <u>I'm not alone.</u>

—anonymous, age 29

I used this book for a school paper. When I turned it in, my teacher thought it was so good that she called my parents!

—Mike, age 9

Ninjas DO NOT kill and stab all day. They aren't "cool" because they can do anything. They are actually highly trained paid-assassins. If they (ninjas) were still around "flipping out and killing people" like Hamburger says, then we would hear about it A LOT more than we usually do. He's so stupid. If Hamburger is going to talk about something he should at least know what he's talking about. He probably doesn't even know what a *shuriken* is. And that's not even the gist of what's wrong with this book. Oh, and by the way, Hamburger—if you're reading this—I'm a sniper. So if you see a red dot appear on your chest, smile, because you'll get to meet somebody who really is "cool," if only for a second. (Sorry if you're crying while reading this, but I don't care.)

—Jeremy C., age 26

Publisher's Note: Parental advisory—immature content. Please do not do anything described in this book. Also, please respect bedtimes *and other people.*

CITADEL PRESS BOOKS are published by

Kensington Publishing corp.
850 Third Avenue
New York, NY 10022

Real Ultimate Power

All Kensington titles, imprints, and distributed lines are available at special quantity discounts for bulk purchases for sales promotions, premiums, fundraising, educational, or institutional use. Special book excerpts or customized printings can also be created to fit specific needs. For details, write or phone the office of the Kensington special sales manager: Kensington Publishing Corp., 850 Third Avenue, New York, NY 10022, attn: Special Sales Department; phone 1-800-221-2647.

CITADEL PRESS and the Citadel logo are Reg. U.S. Pat. & TM Off.

All interior illustrations courtesy James Novy, except pp. 132–35

First printing: July 2004

20 19 18 17 16 15 14 13 12 11 10

Printed in the United States of America

Library of Congress Control Number: 2003113141

ISBN: 0-8065-2569-X

ACKNOWLEDGMENTS

Good morning. I would like to thank my dog Francine, whose real name I will not disclose because of privacy. And I want to thank my baby-sitter, John Fielding, for helping me write this book. He's cool, I guess. Plus, I thank my parents for having sex and making me, but THAT'S ALL. Third, I would like to thank Miek Coccia, Daniel Greenberg, and Jeremie Ruby-Strauss for realizing that a simple kid could teach people about ninjas. (Though, they are always laughing at me—so I don't know what their problem is.) O.K., see ya later!

This book is disgusting.

—Robert's Mom

For the hippos . . .

CONTENTS

APPENDIX AND EXHIBITS   169

LAST WILL AND TESTIMONY

Dear Everybody,

This is my last will and testimony. If you find this book, then you should consider me dead meat. I have left the neighborhood, because I am a true live ninja and I have a destiny—total sweetness. You probably don't understand what that is, because you're an idiot. Everybody I know doesn't understand the complete sweetness of ninjas and it hurts me—you hurt me. But don't get me wrong—I don't want your heads to explode. I forgive you, but I just deserve something cooler.

You can have all of my stuff: my shirt, my beach towel, and that bowl. I don't care. But most importantly, I leave you this book so maybe, just maybe, you can understand the way of the ninja—REAL Ultimate Power.

Farewell dummies,
Robert Hamburger

Do you want to know what REAL Ultimate Power is?
(If yes, then turn the page. If no, then close the book *right now*.)

Do you want to get pumped?

I mean really, *really* pumped?

REAL
Ultimate
Power

The Official Ninja Book

by Robert Hamburger

CITADEL PRESS
Kensington Publishing Corp.
www.kensingtonbooks.com

INTRODUCTION: WHY I WROTE A BOOK ABOUT NINJAS AND STUFF

Have you ever been so pumped that you want to completely flip out? I mean like really *really* flip out. People get pumped about all sorts of things: sports, pets, making out, or motorcycles. Do you want to know what gets me pumped? Ninjas. Ninjas are so sweet, I want to crap my pants.

When I wake up in the morning, I lay in bed for a few hours and practice kicking and punching with my feet and arms. (Don't worry, homey, I'm only practicing.) After that, I go eat breakfast with Mom, like eggs and toast and stuff. Then I go nuts: I throw towels, scream at birds, and spit on the carpet. And THEN after *all* that, my dog Francine and I dress up like ninjas and make forts and fight and French and flip out all day.

You see, I love ninjas so much it hurts, and that's why I made this book about them. I don't know if there are even ninjas anymore, but sometimes I think that there must be, because of the feeling inside me. My parents fight. Just imagine being a ninja.

You could kill anybody you want. And I mean ANYBODY! These guys are sooooo sweet. And do you know why? They flip out and kill people *for no reason at all*. That's awesome! Do you know of anybody else who can do that? Probably not. Your dad couldn't even kill people just because he wanted to. He would go to jail in a second. But ninjas . . . yeah, right! There's no way you could put them in jail. Ninjas are unstoppable and charming. Pirates and Vikings are cool, but they don't go nuts like ninjas. And ninjas have magical powers, too. They can fly. Every human being on the face of the planet wants to fly, and ninjas have been doing it since day one. DAY ONE! And that's a fact. Some ninjas have the power to bio-slime people. It may sound disgusting, but trust me, it's pretty sweet.

I am not attracted to ninjas, personally. But sometimes when I'm lying in the backyard and I'm thinking about ninjas for more than an hour, I pop a boner. Sometimes they're small, but sometimes they're humongous. Mom caught me one time when this happened. She said, "What the heck is going on? What are you doing?" And she chased me around the yard with a rake. When she caught me, she made me lay on my stomach and she stepped on my butt. Mom's pretty big, so it went away real fast. But when she stopped and it came back even bigger, I knew that ninjas were special. These guys are *totally sweet*. Everyday I ask my mom if I can take karate. I say, "Hey Mom, can I take karate?" And she says, "No way! You'll hurt someone." So we compromised on yoga—I start next year. But who cares, I don't need karate—I express myself by screaming and imagining stories about ninjas.

I guess I just want to tell the people of Earth about something totally sweet. I have felt this way all my life. My name is Robert, and this is my book about the coolest guys to ever flip out.

GETTING STARTED: WHY NINJAS?

You might be asking yourself why you should learn about ninjas when there are so many other things to learn about. Personally, I don't understand that question. Ninjas are so awesome. And in case you you've been stuck in the house for the past ten years, ninjas are deadly assassins. For example, they would dress up like a salesman to get into your house and, while they're pretending to sell you something, they would look for holes and cracks to climb into. So then, at night, they would come back and murder you. Most ninjas are in Asian countries, but you can find them just about anywhere. Ninjas have weapons, like ninja stars and the ninja sword.

Ninjas can kill *anyone they want*! They cut off heads ALL the time and don't even think twice about it! These guys are so crazy and awesome that they flip out ALL the time. I heard that there was this ninja who was eating at a diner. And when some dude dropped a spoon, the ninja killed the whole town. And my friend Mark said that he saw a ninja totally uppercut some kid just because the kid opened a window. And that's what I call REAL Ultimate Power!!!!!!!!!!!!!!!!!! If you don't believe that ninjas have REAL Ultimate Power, you better get a life right now or they will chop your head off!!! It's an easy choice, if you ask me. Ninjas are fast, smooth, cool, strong, talented, powerful, and sweet. I love them with all of my body, including my pee-pee.

PART I

Who Are These Guys and What's Their Problem?

A famous warrior won a bunch of battles. He won so many that he started thinking he was too cool to hang out with his old buddies. But one day a hippo bit his shoulder and the warrior needed a simple antidote. So he called everybody he knew, but they were all busy having fun with their dog and everything. So nobody was around to wipe his poor, poor baby butt. Too bad, little baby! Too bad.

—Ancient Chinese Fable

If you were to ask someone six months ago what they thought ninjas were, they'd probably say, "Excuse me. Ninjas? Who cares! Get out of the way—my fucking soaps are on!" Unfortunately, today isn't much different. Most Westerners don't know much about them. There are even stories that ninjas are descended from monsters or demons, but only a baby would believe that. Ninjas came from vaginas, just like everybody else. In this section of my book, I'm going to start out with the basics—who they are, what they do, and other stuff. And then I'll help you to understand total sweetness and appreciate what ninjas have to offer. And later, we'll get into the more complicated stuff, like their history, how to be friends with one, or even how to become one. But first, we need[1] to[2] get[3] pumped.[4]

---

[1] Hey Robert! It's me, John.

[2] What the heck! This is my book. What are you doing here?

[3] Well, I know that I'm only your baby-sitter, but I could help you out with the book, if you like. I'm a student of philosophy and I could make corrections and clear up misunderstandings the reader may have. You'd be surprised how making a few technical distinctions can save a work from an unneeded diarrhea burst.

[4] That's frigg'n disgusting! I don't want that to happen. You can be my editor or something.

The Pump-Up Part:
Some of Mine and Francine's Favorite Movie Scripts

Before we get into the science of ninjas, you need to get pumped, really really pumped. I get my dog, Francine, pretty pumped by telling her stories about ninjas. So I wrote three short movie scripts (by myself) to get your blood hot and crazy. The first film, *Ninja, Please*, introduces the ways of the ninja. The second film, *Ninja Babe*, is sexual. And the last film, *The Ultimate Battle*, introduces the ninja's stupidest opponent. Hopefully, you'll enjoy them as much as I like looking at naked ladies.

Ninja, Please

SCENE 1:
Ninjas walk down the street to go eat some food. They are all wearing black and looking totally sweet. There is some awesome music playing in the background to get the audience really pumped. Then some dude jumps out of nowhere. The ninjas start beating this guy's ass, bad. Then the dude starts trying to run away, but one ninja pulls out a ninja star (ninja weapon) and throws it at the guy. The ninja star cuts the guy's head totally off. The head rolls over near this old dog that looks at the head and barfs all over the place, including on the camera, which is awesome. The ninjas then start flying and everybody starts screaming. Then the scene ends.

SCENE 2:
A ninja is sleeping at his house. Some idiot walks by singing a super annoying song. Then the ninja wakes up super pissed and ready to rock. The guy just keeps walking and singing, while

the ninja starts cutting down a building. When the guy walks by the building, it falls on him. (While the building is falling, a guitar will be wailing hard in the background.) There will be a close-up of the dude's feet sticking out from under the building. The feet explode all over the place, because of blood pressure. Then we see that the ninja was playing the guitar. Then the ninja starts flipping out hard and totally wails on the guitar. Then all these babes start coming out of nowhere and the ninja starts wailing even harder (if that's even possible). Then the camera starts fading out and then explodes.

The End

I thought of this script one night right before bedtime. I got so pumped I almost kicked my mom right in the face!

Ninja Babe

SCENE 1:
There is this super rich, stupid idiot who lives in a humongous house. At his house, this guy has babes lying all over the place. The next scene is hot. The guy takes this super hot babe back to his room to make-out. The audience will think that the hot babe is a normal babe, but, yeah right, she's a ninja. The ninja woman smashes the guy's head like a hairy melon. Then all these dogs come out of nowhere and the ninja woman has to beat the dogs' asses. First, she kicks this one dog right in the nuts. The dog screams and jumps out the window. Then she jumps in the air and kicks two dogs in the nuts at once! Both dogs evaporate. Every time the ninja woman kicks nuts, a guitar squeals hard. Then the ninja woman has to battle the boss dog. The boss dog is huge. Before the boss dog can attack, she uppercuts the boss dog's nuts so hard that he explodes. Then the guitar squeals REALLY hard and explodes.

The End

This script is awesome and that's a fact.

The Ultimate Battle

SCENE 1:

Dark smoke fills the scene and pump-up music slowly gets louder. The audience sees a ninja and his girlfriend eating at a super expensive restaurant. The girlfriend is so hot that steam is coming out of her mouth or hair. Some old idiot is sitting by the couple. The idiot is giving the girlfriend "the eye" and popping, like, sixteen boners. But, the ninja sees the boners and the music really pumps up. The audience knows this guy is dead meat for sure. But, out of nowhere, the old idiot pulls off his jacket to show that he is a pirate with lasers and everything. The ninja is like, "Yeah right, who cares?" and then pops the biggest boner ever, bigger than the biggest, blackest boner alive. The ninja's boner smashes the entire restaurant. And every single one of the pirate's boners explodes while making whistling sounds. The ninja looks back at his girlfriend. She smiles and they pork.

The End

While writing this script, I head-butt my dog so hard that we both screamed.

If You Don't Believe That Ninjas Exist, You're a Moron: The Proof

I bet you're pretty pumped right now, because I know I am. But you also might be thinking that ninjas don't exist and those scripts were just magical fantasies, but you're wrong and stupid, if you ask me. Here's absolute proof of that they really do exist.

Though you never know when somebody is a frigg'n liar, I think my best friend Mark's stories are true. One night, I slept over at his house and he told me that for the last week a ninja was hanging out in his backyard, behind the shed. I was like, "Yeah, right." So we waited until Mark's parents went to bed to check out the ninja. We sneaked out without making too much noise and the night air was intense. And to tell you the truth, I had never been that pumped before in my life. We didn't think we'd make it to the shed alive, but we did. Mark almost died from the jogging—so we rested in front of the shed for a while. But out of nowhere, we heard this huge BANG behind the shed. Mark was like, "Holy CRAP!" and a little piece of poop seeped out of my butthole. Then we frigg'n booked back towards Mark's house. I was so pumped and excited that I jumped right through the living room window and cut my legs and arm. Mark's parents flew out of bed screaming and yelling. Mark got an erection and got grounded, and I got sent home. But I didn't care about any of that crap, because I knew right then that Mark was telling the truth—ninjas exist.

So if you don't believe that ninjas exist, you might get your ass beat and/or killed! If some book says that ninjas don't exist and you believe it, then you're[5] a[6] moron.[7]

---

[5] Hey Robert, that was a really good crack at it—you should submit it to the school paper or something. While you are completely correct in stating that ninjas exist, you are not justified in concluding that ninjas exist from your argument: that huge bang might have been a raccoon, or your drunken father. So I've added a little argument here to support your claim.

The Ontological Proof of Ninjas

When we talk about the ninja, we are talking about the sweetest being ever—that is, we are talking about the being than which nothing sweeter can be conceived. So, when we conceive of the ninja in our mind, we conceive of the being than which nothing sweeter can be conceived. But consider this: Is it sweeter to exist only in the mind or to exist both in the mind and in reality—outside the mind? Certainly, it is much sweeter to exist also in reality—flipping out and wailing on guitars is much sweeter when someone is *actually* doing it. So when we conceive of the sweetest being ever, we are conceiving of the being that exists both in the mind and in reality. Since the ninja is that being than which nothing sweeter can be conceived and that being exists in the mind *and in reality*, the ninja exists in reality. Thus the ninja exists—**John, ed**.

[6] John, that was totally sweet. I think I just crapped my pants.

[7] Me, too.

Basic Facts About These Guys

Now that you know that ninjas really do exist, you can shut your mouth. In this chapter, we will learn about the REAL ninja, not the cartoon kind who kills only when they have to. Let's begin with the facts.

1. Ninjas are mammals.[8] Ninjas are hot-blooded hairy animals who don't lay eggs. They live in the woods or in dojos or in houses like you and me. They graze. Baby ninjas eat blood-milk. Basically, their mating season is whenever they want, which is awesome.[9]

2. Ninjas fight *ALL* the time. *Ninja* means *"fight"* in German and Mexican. It is the ninja's nature to always fight. If they stop fighting, they start to lose power or energy, and I don't want that to ever happen.

3. The purpose of the Ninja is to flip out and kill people. Think about the time that you got so pumped you couldn't believe it. Now, multiply that times about a billion. That's how pumped a ninja is ALL THE TIME. If a regular person ever got that pumped, they'd have to take Ritalin or something.[10] But the

---

[8] Encyclopedia Britannica, volume N.

[9] I went to check your sources in the Encyclopedia Britannica. I guess someone ripped out several pages in the "N" section. If you know where they might be, let me know. I'm not saying that you did it or anything. I just want to make sure you understand that it's not cool to rip up books you don't like or disagree with. How about we just leave the facts as they are until we find those missing pages—**John, ed.**

[10] Check out **Exhibit A** in the *Appendix and Exhibits* to see a rough draft of a paper I did while on Ritalin and then the final draft, **Exhibit B,** when I got off Ritalin.

bottom line is that ninjas basically exist to kill morons who can't keep their mouths shut. (That might mean you.)

4. Ninjas hang out in dojos (a lot). Dojos are kinda like bars where ninjas go to relax and/or meet babes. You can do anything you want at the dojo. If you want to eat a whole pizza by yourself, go ahead. Or if you just want to goof around, no problem. I saw one dojo in a magazine where they had drinking fountains of pop—that's great, if you ask me.

5. Ninjas hang out with other ninjas or, as Mom says, only with "really down-to-earth kids." But she's full of BULLCRAP! Ninjas hang out with the sweetest of people. Throughout the ages, ninjas have hung out with kings, popes, jesters, boxers, vampires, and geniuses. But most of the time, ninjas just hang out with their clan, which is a bunch of buddies who either live in the same neighborhood or whose moms know each other.

Questions That Kids in the Neighborhood Ask Me

> **Did You Know?**
> Ninjas made killing cool. Before them, everybody was like, "Killing? Yeah right!" But now everybody's like, "Sweet."

Because there's just so much to know about ninjas, I could speak about them all day, but I won't. Nevertheless, kids in my neighborhood ask me a lot of questions about ninjas, AND THEY'RE ALWAYS THE SAME ONES, which makes me think that you might be asking yourself the same questions too. I'm going to deal with this crap right now.

Q: Why is everyone so obsessed about ninjas?
A: Ninjas are the ultimate paradox. On the one hand they don't give a crap, but on the other hand, ninjas are very careful[11] and[12] precise.[13]

---

[11] Not bad. Looks like you're starting to understand different types of paradoxes. But there is another paradox you may have missed. You say that ninjas flip out, but many contemporary philosophers take that to mean ninjas lose their cool. They argue that since ninjas lose their cool *they aren't cool*, but you've obviously shown that ninjas are very cool or *totally sweet*. The problem with their argument is the equivocation of the word "cool." Sometimes, we take a word in a true sentence and change the meaning of it for more interesting results. In accepting the new meaning, we leave behind the meaning that originally lead us to believe that the sentence was true. Furthermore, we often believe that the new sentence is true, because we think that it's the same sentence as the original. Take the sentence, "Ninjas don't keep their *cool*," which means that ninjas don't keep an *easy going temperament*, which is obviously true. But, one might take the meaning of "cool" in the above sentence to be *their ability to be cool*.

Q: I heard that ninjas are always cruel or mean. What's their problem?

A: Whoever told you that is a total liar. Just like other mammals, ninjas can be mean OR totally awesome.

Q: What do ninjas do when they're not cutting off heads or flipping out?

A: Most of their free time is spent flying, but sometimes they stab. (Ask Mark if you don't believe me.)

Q: Why do your parents fight all the time?

A: It's not because they're ninjas or anything. I think it's because my dad probably isn't my real dad. You see, I sometimes think that a ninja secretly had vaginal sex with my mom so that he would be my real father. In fact, it has to be true, because I feel it in my heart. My real father, the ninja, may be traveling all over the world killing people whenever he wants, fighting everyday, going berserk and/or flipping out. What would he do if he could see me now? Dear Dad, do you think of me when you're flipping out and killing trillions of people? Do you pop boners about having a son? When are we going to hang out, Dad? That would be crazy if we both had a psychic connection and always popped boners at the exact same time. That would explain a lot, I think.

On the latter interpretation of "cool," ninjas don't keep their ability to be cool, which leads us to believe that ninjas aren't cool or aren't totally sweet. So, one might be tempted to believe that since "ninjas don't keep their cool" is true, the sentence "ninjas aren't cool" is true. But there is no reason to accept that ninjas can't keep *their ability to be cool*, if we believe that ninjas don't keep *an easy going temperament*. An easy going temperament and an ability to be cool are two independent properties. That is to say, an object may have one property without having the other. We only believe that the truth of the sentence "ninjas don't keep their cool" leads to the truth of the sentence "ninjas aren't cool" if we equivocate the meaning of cool in the former sentence with the meaning of cool in the latter case, which is, all together, an unjustified move. So ninjas don't keep their cool *and* ninjas are cool.—**John, ed.**

[12] John, I don't understand what you said, but it sounds pretty frigg'n sweet. Keep doing it, 'cause it makes my book sound deep.

[13] Hell yeah, dude. Since ninjas are so mysterious, philosophers have been arguing about them for ages. I'm sure I can find more stuff like this.

Q: What's with their boners anyway?
A: It is one of their strongest/hottest weapons. See the weapons section, later on.

Q: Why is your mom so crabby?
A: Well, it's just me and Mom at home all day, and she told me that she got menopause because I talk about "those fucking ninjas all the fucking time." She says that if I go near her, I'll catch menopause, too! And I don't need that kind of stuff[14] in[15] my[16] life.[17]

Q: How do you know all this stuff about ninjas?
A: I am a ninja-in-waiting and have been chosen, I think, to be a real ninja when I'm big enough.

Q: Robert, why are you such a faggot?
A: Let me ask you this: How would you like to die this afternoon? I'll smoke your entire life like a cigar or pipe! I'll cut your face in half!

---

[14] Did she really say that?—**John, ed.**

[15] Yep.

[16] Dude, your mom's a dick!

[17] I told you!

The Official Ninja Code of Honor

Ninjas are more than just a bunch of facts. They're real. And they have a special code they live by. A long time ago, there was the First Ninja, who knew how frigg'n sweet he was, and that everyone else in the world would try to be like him. But he also knew that some people would get it wrong and ruin EVERY-THING. So he wrote down a bunch of crap. This way, future people could understand REAL Ultimate Power and use it only for Total Sweetness. After he wrote The Ninja Code of Honor, he mysteriously nailed it to the door of a huge church, so everyone would see it. This is what it said:

The Ninja Code of Honor

I, the First Ninja, had a dream that one day everyone could be Totally Sweet and flip out, but also I had a nightmare that one day some frigg'n idiot would screw everything up, so I here do declare that The Ninja Code of Honor be that which every ninja sets himself out of stone by and into and, hopefully, in four score and seven days, everybody will know what REAL Ultimate Power is. So let me tell you my story, so you can live like a REAL ninja.

In the beginning was Total Sweetness, and Total Sweetness was with the Ninja, and Total Sweetness was the Ninja. And when people saw this Ninja they freaked, because he was glowing and everything. And then some idiot came up to him and asked, "What's your problem?" And the Ninja said . . .

"When in the course of humans, it becomes necessary for People to dissolve and/or melt into one another, which is disgusting, there comes one completely awesome guy, me, who will form a more perfect union of chopping off heads and looking Totally Sweet."

"What are you talking about?" asked the idiot.

"Never kill anybody for a reason. This is the meat-and-potatoes of honor. Honor is the ability to kill anybody anytime without giving a crap. And that's a fact.

"Be buddies with someone forever if you say that you'll be friends, 'cause it's pretty frigg'n lame when somebody pretends to be your friend and invites you over to play ninja fight, and you set up the fort for your best friend and it's your turn to be the ninja and you get pretty frigg'n pumped and throw his cat against the wall ('cause you're pumped) and his mom screams and picks you up and takes you outside and drops you in the front yard AND NOW he hasn't talked to you for three years, 'cause he says he's in the army, but you see him next door in his bedroom eating pizza or playing basketball with girls. So remember, a real ninja hangs out with his best friends and doesn't ignore friends just because they got too pumped.

"Be completely and utterly sweet. A lot of people forget this while flipping out and just act like idiots, like this one kid who lives down the street and thinks he's so bad because he saw some lady getting a pap smear and brags about it *all the time*.

"And make the most of your life. If you live life passively, you are wasting a precious gift. Our time on Earth is finite and valuable—to carelessly waste it is a crime of the mind and soul. But death is a gift, too, and you should deal with honor and Total Sweetness by The Ninja Code of Honor.

"Now let this be a warning to you and your buddies. If you want to be a ninja, you must follow these rules or you will get your ass beat bad."

Thanks a lot,
The First Ninja

Fighting Styles

Different ninjas fight with different styles. No single style is the best, but some are obviously stupider than others. A lot of people say that ninjitsu isn't that great, but I'd like to see them say that while sitting next to a ninja. Just imagine yourself introducing one of those guys to a ninja. "Oh hello, this is my friend Mark. Mark, this is a ninja. My friend Mark here thinks that ninjas are pretty stupid. He thinks that you ninjas can't do anything." Oh, man. Just imagine the ninja sitting there drinking coffee with one hand and gripping some ninja stars with the other. Your friend would be so frigg'n scared. Here are some other fighting styles:

Karate

Karate is retarded. It's basically aerobics with pajamas. If you want to be a real ninja you don't *have* to take it. Most people who join karate only do it because their parents make them. It's basically for people who need an attitude adjustment—that's all. Karate's basic moves are breaking wood; some kicks; up, up, down, down, left right, left right, B, A, select, start; and other stuff—I can't remember right now.

Yoga

A lot kids in my neighborhood say that yoga doesn't have anything to do with ninjas, but that's a bunch of bull crap! I mean, these are the same kids that think a lady's period is when the lining of the uterus is shed through the vagina. Like I'm really going to believe them about yoga! Yoga is the most effective fighting style ever. If you stretch hard enough, you probably don't have to fight anybody. One time, I did the spits without warning and some people started running. It's awesome. The main move is the splits.

Pressure Points

Sometimes if a ninja is relaxing and doesn't feel like getting all sweaty, they'll use pressure points on an enemy. Pressure points are one of the coolest ways to gently beat somebody's ass. You could just be sitting there, relaxing and watching TV, pretending you're not going to completely beat the crap of somebody and then WHAM! you softly touch their wrist and they go to sleep forever! It's like you've got so much power that you don't need to waste energy on someone you hate. One of the greatest pressure points ever is the touch of death. I mean, can you believe that ninjas can kill a person without cutting or strangling them? It almost doesn't make sense. Almost. With just a simple caress, a ninja could end a human life. And it doesn't happen right away— so no one will ever figure out who did it. Here's what happens. A ninja touches the back of some dude's head. Then the back of the head sends a signal to the stomach. Then the stomach sends a signal to the liver. And then, finally, the liver tells the heart something. And the guy dies! So if somebody says to you, "Hello Sir (or Madam), would you like me to rub the back of your head?" You should probably say, "No," or "No thank you," because they might be a ninja, completely willing to kill you, but just too tired to get all crazy about it.

Menopause

Menopause is pretty powerful and gives someone a mustache. If you know anybody who uses this style, you should probably just stay upstairs. The main moves are slapping with rolled up maga-zines, screaming power, single- or double-handed spanking, and hot flashes.

Meditation

Some people ask me how ninjas can be harmonious with nature when they're constantly kicking people in the nuts. Well, they just can—so don't worry about it. They mediate and think about what they've done. During meditation, ninjas will spend hours away from TV and friends. This is when they learn about themselves, mainly reflecting on deep questions like, "Why can't you act normal and stop embarrassing your mother and me?" and, "Why can't you stop acting like a fucking retard?" And, after they're done, they're allowed to come back downstairs and watch TV.

Judo

Judo is pretty lame. It's basically a self-defense style. So when they have tournaments, there's never a winner, because nobody

ever makes the first move. The main moves are not doing anything and waiting. It's stupid.

A Ninja Makes a Telephone Call

Guy: Hello.
Ninja: Hey.
Guy: What's going on?
Ninja: Nothing, just hanging out. What about you?
Guy: I'm just hanging out, too.
Ninja: That's cool.
Guy: I gotta go.
Ninja: Really?
Guy: Yeah, see ya later.
Ninja: O.K., bye.

Some Frigg'n Badass Ninja Weapons

You don't know crap unless you know about ninja weapons, which are pretty amazing, if you ask anybody. Even though these guys are infinitely sweet without them, somehow weapons make them sweeter, in a paradoxical kind of way.

Ninja Stars

Ninja stars, or Chinese stars, are one of their coolest weapons. These can really mess up someone's life. Ninjas love them because they are small enough to fit in a backpack or lunch bag. Oh hello, would you like to steal my lunch? How would you like to see out of a tube for the rest of your life! BOOM! That would be so frigg'n sweet. Just imagine some moron saying that crap to your face and having a boatload of ninja stars in your pocket. He'd wish his parents never even thought about making love. That guy would be sitting meat. Then I'd go over to his house and rip out his dog's hair and spit all over the place. And then I'd make love to his mother's butt, while everybody in the nation watched. Take my lunch—yeah, right! I'll bite your face off.

Ninja Sword

The ninja sword is shorter than the samurai sword, but that doesn't mean the samurai sword is better. There are big debates about which sword is the best—conferences and stuff—but people who believe that the ninja sword isn't the sweetest are stupid idiots. They put their ninja sword in a long pocket on their back so that their hands are free for climbing up dojos and stuff like that. The ninja sword is mainly used on necks, but it can also be used on arms, legs, and stomachs. The guy who invented it is probably pretty cool (and pretty rich, if you ask me).[18]

Guitar

The guitar is the ninja's trumpet. He uses it as a warning that danger is near and he's ready to rock. If a ninja's finger merely brushes up against a guitar, a humongous wail will happen. No other mammals can wail as hard. It has something to do with magic. I asked Dad if he would get me a guitar for Christmas, and he said he would buy me one if I ran away.

Boner

The boner is the ninja's hottest weapon. A ninja can pop thousands of them if they get super pumped. Some studies even show that a ninja can pop more than a million boners, if they need to.

---

[18] Personally, I think that the ninja sword is the sweetest weapon. It's a bold statement, I know. Though, I could be an advocate of ninja stars someday, but it really depends on the circumstances.

They can be used on babes[19] or morons. Ninjas can slam or slap their opponent or girlfriend with it. The boner is also used to help balance when they are tree-waiting. I remember my first boner. I was looking through my neighbor's window and could see some lady changing her panties and everything. But check this out, behind her on the bed I could see this big orange cat licking its nutsack. And BOOM! My pants inflated like an air bag. Mom busted into the room, and was like, "What the heck are you doing?" And I was like, "Nothing." And she was like, "Yeah, right."

[19] Francine and I were super bored one day and tried to go find some naked ladies. We waited outside this drugstore till we saw this guy come out. We were like, "Dude, buy us a *Playboy*?" and he was like, "Got money?" So we gave him ten bucks and waited outside. But then, he busted out of the store and said, "You guys stay right here. They just called the cops, and you're busted." When he went back inside the store, we frigg'n ran. Francine ran down one street and I ran down another, I can't remember which. I was running for like TEN MINUTES STRAIGHT. But then, out of nowhere, this car started flying down the road, and I jumped right into a bunch of bushes and scratched up my face and legs and everything. I hid there till nightfall. Francine ran straight home and waited till I got back. We were so freaked out that we both slept in the same sleeping bag that night.

Skills Non-Ninjas Only Dream of Having

Did You Know?

Ninjas can only climb ladders backwards because of their huge boners. So they invented the catapult to get themselves into people's backyards and onto roofs.

Flying

Ninjas fly all the time, because it's cheap and easy. Not like birds, but more like hovercrafts, like they're floating in the pool, but in air. All they need to do is start thinking about knives and necks, and they start to rise.

Invisibility

Being invisible would be pretty great, if you ask me. You could do anything! Suppose you were invisible and there is some kid who used to like you, but doesn't anymore because you don't know why, and he's going through puberty, and just when he's about to go to a fancy wedding or something, you sprinkle pubes all over his shirt, and it screws up the entire ceremony.

Smoke Screen

This is for ninjas who can't get invisible for some reason.

Bio-slime

This is used for sticking to walls or for just freaking out the ladies. The slime comes out of their armpits, feet, and mouth. They spray when they get pumped.

Trapping

Ninja traps can be used for catching people. And then they can either scare their victim or just kill them, basically it's up to the ninja. For example, if a ninja wants to trap a bunch of people at once, he could put a huge net in the street and cover it with leaves and twigs. Then when a bus comes, he would pull the rope and BOOM, he's got them. The ninja would tip the bus over so everybody falls out into a huge tarp. Then the police would come see this bus just hanging from a tree, and they'd start screaming because they couldn't understand what was going on. And the ninja would take the big bag of people and toss it into a lake where everybody inside would try to get out, but instead they'd end up scratching and kicking each other. And the ninja would sit on top and spread a blanket over the bubbling bag and enjoy a picnic with his friends and neighbors. The sun would keep the food warm, and they would look at each and know that everything's going to be okay.

Porking

Ninjas are the toughest lovers ever! They are romantic and classy, making them a great opponent in any mating ritual. And after some wine, they spray nectar on their territory to attract mates, which usually works.

X-ray vision

With X-ray vision, a ninja can see through anything. A ninja uses this skill mostly for spying on victims or checking out women's crotches. Ninjas can relax on a park bench during the weekend and look at vaginas all day, and nobody will ever know.

Top Eleven Reasons Why Ninjas Kill People

Picture an awesome field with tall grass and sunlight. Some deer are talking in the corner, but it's nothing big. Then there's you—face down and naked—all because you couldn't shut your frigg'n mouth. A lot of people die from ninjas. I mean A LOT. And they all probably died for different reasons. And if you were to ask eleven different people what they thought about ninjas, you'd probably get one answer: "Totally sweet." But that doesn't mean if you ask eleven different ninjas why they killed somebody, they'll give you the same answer. Here are some reasons why a ninja might kill you:

1. Talking crap about somebody
2. Being stupid
3. Being retarded
4. Telling a teacher that somebody has fireworks in their pocket when it doesn't HAVE ANYTHING TO DO WITH YOU
5. Telling secrets about your best buddy to get people to like you
6. Liking someone your friend likes
7. Saying that you like somebody, but deep inside, you don't
8. Or liking somebody and telling them and everything, but as soon as they start liking you, you stop liking them, 'cause you're almost fully retarded
9. Giving your son dish detergent and a vacuum for Christmas, which doesn't make sense, when all he really wanted was a robot that turned into a gun

10. Giving somebody homework *on Halloween*

11. Telling somebody that you're going to come over and spend the night, and they wait for like three hours with the phone in their hand, and they even pooped in a bowl so they didn't miss you in case you knocked, but, guess what, you never showed up, and they call your house, and your mom picks up the phone and is like, "I don't know where he is. I'll tell him you called. So please stop calling." And when they see you the next day at school, you're like, "Oh. Sorry, I forgot."

Japan
(Where Ninjas Basically Came From)

Just imagine yourself being a ninja back in the olden days. It would just be you and a bunch of animals riding around the forest, and you could have your own castle with bears as guards that change shifts and everything. But, best of all, ninjas would be everywhere. A lot of people get the wrong idea about ninjas, because the only people to write about them were the ruling families of medieval Japan. Since they didn't like ninjas AT ALL, they would talk huge amounts of crap about them, which isn't fair when you think about it. They hated ninjas so much that back then, if somebody even mentioned the word "ninja," they got their ass beat bad. And the only other people who wrote about them in the olden days were the British, and in case you haven't heard, they were dicks—big time.

Basically, ninjas came from Japan, which is screaming distance from China. Every single person in Japan gets to learn karate, even the fat ones. It's like a fantasy. Japanese people use chopsticks for forks and use forks as pocket-weapons. But, before there were ninjas in Japan, there were samurais. I *used* to be really into samurais. I thought they were so great and everything. I couldn't even do my homework or finish dessert. I would talk about samurais ALL THE TIME. People couldn't stand being around me, and I don't blame them. I refer to that time as my "crazy days."

Mark used to be into samurais back then, too. We would stay up all night thinking about them, and we wouldn't even have to talk. We'd just be sitting on the floor, thinking about how sweet they were. Then, Mark and I would pretend to be in an ancient samurai's bedroom fighting demons. But after a while he started to wear cologne and hair spray, which didn't make sense, because samurais didn't have access to that kind of stuff. He stopped caring about the details. And pretty soon, he stopped caring about samurais all together, which was crazy! And when I'd call and talk to him about samurais, he always had to go, because he said his mom needed his help, but I never heard her in the background. I'm not into samurais any more, though. I'm moving on, putting my life in order and my toys away. I'm growing up, and it's showing everyday. I was too scared before, but now, I'm not afraid. I'll stare people right down. And they always look away. And before samurais, I was into zombies. And before that, it[20] was[21] catapults.[22]

---

[20] Man, dude, you remind me of when I was obsessed with fire engines. I loved them so much that I wanted to be one when I grew up. Isn't that stupid?—**John, ed.**

[21] No, it's not! If you really love something, then why not?

[22] Maybe you're right. It's too bad that no matter how much you love something, whether it's a rock band or a video game or ninjas, and you tell yourself that you're always gonna love them, one day you just won't. Even if you still want to like that thing, whatever it is, it begins to lose its magic. And by the time you realize that you might not always love catapults, or whatever, it has already begun.

Who Would Win?
Ninjas vs. Anybody

Since ninjas fight all the time, they have a lot of enemies. So here, I have collected a list of ninjas' most formidable opponents and will talk about how bad ninjas would kill them in a REAL fight.

Vikings

Viking are pretty cool, but you can't understand them, because they only speak through plundering and raping. Ninjas don't have anything to steal, and if a Viking tries to rape a ninja, oh man, that Viking would get a surprise—how about a six-foot-boner-uppercut?

Pirates

These guys are the crap de la crap. They think that they're pretty sweet with the boats and lasers, but they really aren't, if you ask me. Number one, they can only use their magic on water. So basically, they are stupid and boring on land. And number two, they could only beat a ninja if the ninja had the flu, chicken pox, measles, mumps, and A.D.D. all at once. And that would probably never happen.

Moms

Moms are one of the ninjas' arch enemies. They always try to make ninjas clean up messes no matter how messy *they* are. Moms have screaming power and level nine spanking, which makes them pretty lethal. But ninjas have level forty-five spanking defense. So moms are pretty useless against ninjas, which is a good thing. Nevertheless, if a ninja is winning against a mom, the mom can send a mammogram to other moms in the neighborhood for backup.

Fairies

All fairies want to do is sprinkle magic sauce on you to make you fly. AND THAT'S BULLCRAP!

Knights

Knights are pretty charming and polite, which may cause jealousy and anger in the ninja, making him react in strange ways, like accidentally slapping a cousin in the mouth because he got a home run and you're too fat to get to first base. But if a ninja realizes that sometimes other people are better than them at certain things, they'll be able to beat a knight's ass correctly.

Baby-sitters

There's no doubt that a ninja would beat a baby-sitter's ass real bad, but baby-sitters are super weird. This, I know. Because I'm not allowed over to Mark's house anymore and Mom went back to work to "get the fuck away from me," Mom got me a baby-sitter named John. He's pretty cool. He gets me and Francine beef jerky and he listens to my ninja stories, but he's really into Ancient Greek culture I guess—playing video games and wearing diapers and stuff. One time, he bent over to pick up a cup of water, and I saw a diaper under his pants. I asked, "What the heck is that?" That's how he expresses himself, he told me. Then he told me a story about this one day last year when he showed up at a day care wearing a diaper and a note that said, "I'm retarded. Please change my diaper." The day care took the note at face value and started to change him, but they called the police when they took the diaper off and saw an erection. Now he can't get a real job except for baby-sitting.

Teachers

These people are bitches or assholes. A teacher would be like, "Yo, stop talking and do your work." And WHAM! A ninja would cut their mouth off so fast they wouldn't hear it coming. Oh man, that would be great. I'd pay a billion bucks to see stuff like that on TV. Homework? Yeah, right! How about a mouth full of ninja stars?

In conclusion, a ninja could kill anybody, if[23] they[24] really[25] wanted[26] to.[27]

---

[23] *Robert!*

[24] What, Mom!

[25] *Why are you always writing this crap?! You only talk about flipping out and killing people and that's no good! How would you like it if somebody killed you?*

[26] I don't care.

[27] *What?! I am going to tell your Dad and he's gonna beat your ass! Write some nice things right now until your father gets home!*

Some Nice Things:
A Nice Poem

Some nice hippos share.
Everybody likes them.
They like everybody.
They live in a clean house
With nice carpet.
And none of them scream
Or hurt people.

But guess what . . .
This one kid starts talking a bunch of crap about the hippos,
like they don't have brains and they eat chicken vomit and stuff
like that, which is BULLCRAP because the hippos weren't
doing anything. They were just hanging out and THAT'S ALL.

But,
The hippos don't flip out and kill him.
The hippos begin to share
And be nice,
Which is pretty mature.[28]

But guess what . . .
The same kid thinks the hippos are a bunch of wimps,
because they don't do anything. So he starts speaking even
more crap, which is disgusting. And everybody in the
neighborhood starts to think that the hippos REALLY ARE
little diaper babies without brains.

---

[28] *I like this part, Robert. See how good it is to be nice?*

But,
The hippos don't care.
They know they're special.
And no kid can take that away.
So, in a nice way,
The hippos beat the kid's ass.
Their arms turn into knives
And they cut his hair and head off.
Nobody ever messed with them again,
Because they were nice
And they[29] shared.[30]

---

[29] Dude, I think your Dad pulled in the driveway. You'd better get of here! **—John, ed.**

[30] Robert!!!! Get down here right now! Did you honestly think that you could get away with making a poem like this, writing about nice things and making them bad? That's wrong and you know it! What kind of hippos kill people? And they were nice hippos, too! Why can't you be nice and normal? I know why—you're retarded. Well, you know what? I can get loco, too. How about getting your ass beat with balloons? Will that work, hombre?

PART II

The REAL History of Ninjas

> *Two women claimed to be the mother of the same kid. So the king said, "Since you're both the mom, I'll rip him into two strips." The women happily agreed. So the king walked over to the kid who said, "Give it to me. I'm crazy." But then, the king looked toward heaven and realized that this kid was AWESOME. So he took him as a pupil and together, they beat the crap out of both moms.*
>
> —Ancient Chinese Fable

History began with the ninja and will end with the ninja in a humongous explosion with arms and legs laying in the street and melted trees and everybody will be like, "Holy CRAP!" and the ninjas will be like, "We told you," and then Jesus will be like, "You guys should have listened," and buildings and planets will explode, and a bunch of ninjas will just be hanging out, chilling. But before that, ninjas did a bunch of stuff—so here it is, in[31] recorded[32] form.[33]

---

[31] *Robert, when are you going to stop this ninja crap?*

[32] But Mom, I'm expressing myself!

[33] *Who ever told you to express yourself?*

Time Line of Ninja History
(Through Time and Space)

8,000,000,000,000 B.C.	First Ninja ever.
Day One	Ninjas start flying and the whole world craps its pants.
6,500,000,000,000 B.C.	Ninjas discover flipping out and, thus, God gives them dominion over everything Totally Sweet.
3,000 B.C.	Ninjas invent magic spells for invisibility, sticking to walls, and bio-slime.
0	Three wise ninjas bring baby Jesus ninja stars, a guitar, and a hot babe.
200 A.D.	Some ninja discovers America by popping a boner so long that it actually touches a beach in Hawaii. Apparently, they kept some sand from the incident inside a tube in some Chinese country. This is where the term "tube steak" comes from.
440 A.D.	Two ninjas kill an entire squadron of pirates and don't even think twice about it.
600 A.D.	For some old queen's birthday, sixty thousand ninjas wail on their guitars and kill a country.
1253 A.D.	Ninjas stop an illegal shipment of camel toe across the Sahara.
1500 A.D.	Ninjas start appearing in Japan, hard.
1945 A.D.	A ninja kills an entire class of eighth graders because some kid *had* to mouth off.

1986 A.D. A ninja breaks world records all over the planet when he porks five hundred hot babes at once.

1997 A.D. One time, my cousins came over. They were chasing each other around in the living room and ran out of the house without closing the door. Dad went nuts and started screaming "CLOSE THE . . ." and I thought, *Cool, my relatives are going to see how crazy my dad is.* But no. He turned his yelling into a song as he sang the word, "DOOOROOOOOROOOOOOORRRRR!" Everybody loved it. Even my aunts. If they weren't there, it would have been different. People would have suffered.

1998 A.D. A teacher or somebody elected me to go and represent the school in the Olympics. It was the one time people were really nice to me. Everybody cheered for me, which is probably why I won all the contests! I won the running and jumping and basketball and other stuff. It was probably the best day of my life, except I couldn't understand much of what the other contestants said and their eyes were so far apart—which was weird, but in a comfortable way. Then I had to go home, and Dad took away all my trophies, 'cause he said they were an embarrassment. According to HIM, I'm not allowed back. It's like when I do something good, it's bad. And when I do something bad, that's bad, too!

1999 A.D. A ninja stops evil businessmen from demolishing a nursing home by popping a six-foot boner for charity.

2000 A.D. I was telling this ninja story to Mom while she was sleeping because that's the only time she'll listen, and I got pumped and slobbered on her blanket, and she sat up and walked upstairs AND GOT ME A DOG THE NEXT DAY! My dog's name is Francine. I love her. Since dog brains aren't that big—maybe the size of a potato chip—I'm not sure they can do uppercuts or spin-kicks, but I know they can French.

2001 A.D.   One time me and Dad were eating with my aunt and cousins. And when my cousin reached for the ketchup, he accidentally hit a tall glass of orange pop and it spilled all over my crotch. I was wearing white jeans. Everybody in the entire restaurant started laughing their asses off, but nobody laughed louder than my dad. He laughed so hard his face turned purple. I didn't say anything, though. I just sat there and, for the first time in my life, I couldn't finish my meal. But later, when I got home, John showed me how to hide a ninja star in a diaper. So it turned out to be a pretty sweet day.

2002 A.D.   Ninjas help free China from Tibet and bunch of crabby monks.

2003 A.D.   I got my first job. My neighbor pays me to chase him when he doesn't feel like jogging that hard. He says it helps him keep in shape, but I just like it when he starts to slow down and I get to scratch his face.

2004 A.D.   This is when I went to camp for a month. It was only supposed to be a week, but Mom never came[34] to[35] pick[36] me[37] up.[38]

---

[34] Mom, do you love me?

[35] *Of course I love you! You're my son!*

[36] But Mom, what if I weren't your son? Would you still love me then?

[37] *Probably not.*

[38] Oh.

History of Holidays

Did You Know?

For the last couple weeks, Mom's been putting salt licks in the back yard to attract deer. Every couple days, the salt is basically gone. She thinks the deer are going crazy back there, but it's just me and Francine eating it after everybody goes to bed.

The holidays are the one time that large groups of people come together in the same room, and a ninja can kill them all at once. A ninja could make a Christmas tree out of razor blades, and you know the rest of the story. Here are a few historical accounts of how ninjas changed the way regular people think about Halloween, Easter, and Christmas.

Halloween

Wolves are screaming all over the place, and the moon is going nuts. Something's going to happen, but nobody knows what. Kids are running around the alleys wearing stuff like costumes and monster masks. Then a couple of them reach this old house. It's huge. Inside the house, there's this really old guy yelling at himself in the mirror. (He's a maniac.) Outside, the kids look at each other, smile, and knock on the door. Candy. The old guy puts on a shirt to cover up the scar on his sweaty chest. Then he stomps to the kitchen and grabs a bowl of chocolates. The door slides open and the kids see the candy, and it looks so good. But when some kid reaches out to take a piece, the old guy grabs his wrist and the kid looks up and BOOM, the old guy slaps him in the mouth. But the kid doesn't take his eye off the chocolates. The old guy then drops a tiny piece of chocolate in the bag, and little bit of drool falls out of the boy's mouth. The next kid walks up, and she gets hit, too! But the kids keep coming back, because they need that candy. And the old guy keeps smacking the kids, even though he isn't their dad. But out of nowhere, this huge mystery kid dressed in pure black appears at the door. He's awesome. Everybody turns around, because he washes his clothes in pure cologne. Then it's his turn and when the old guy grabs HIS wrist, the mystery kid pulls his wrist back, hard. The old guy starts freaking out. "What the heck?" he whispers to himself in slow-mo. Then the guy steps outside his house and tries to grab the mystery kid's wrist again and the kid whips his hand right back and slams it in his pocket. The other kids see what's happening. So they bum rush the crazy maniac and start biting him all over, except his crotch, and they stuff handfuls of candy in his throat, so no one can hear his blood-gargle. Then it's over. The kids stay in the house all year, redecorating it and making it into a badass fort with secret passages and everything. As for the kid in black, he went back to trick-or-treating because he wasn't even close to being done.

Easter

It was Easter eve, and there's this kid who is so excited about tomorrow's egg hunt. But his mom says to him, "When you go to bed, stay there, because if the Easter bunny is hiding the eggs and he sees you downstairs, he'll scratch your eyes out. Just stay up there, because he's still an animal, and he can't ever change." Then the kid skips dessert and books upstairs. He goes straight to bed—no problem. But later that night, it gets real dark and foggy, and then there's a rumbling downstairs. Some plates break. The kid covers his entire body with a blanket, and he almost can't breathe. Then, there is a scratching at the door, and the kid blacks out for like five seconds. He busts out of bed and pushes his dresser against the door and throws towels over the windows. The claws keep scratching and scratching at the door, and the kid stuffs the corner of his pillow into his mouth and screams. But then it stops. And when the kid wakes up, it's daytime and he opens up his door and looks around. And there, on the door, is a little tiny scratch mark, like something a rabbit would do.

Christmas

Alright, the scene opens up with snow everywhere. There's yelling in the background, but the audience won't know what's going on. Then Santa jumps out of the snow and just starts screaming at the elves. And they scream right back. There will then be some mumbling. Apparently, there's fog and nobody can get their presents or anything, and kids' hearts are getting all twisted up because they need those fucking toys so bad, even if they had a lot already and there are some kids who don't have any, or at least any cool ones, 'cause their parents are assholes or something. But regardless of everything, there's hope. And that hope is in the shape of a real live ninja. But there is trouble, too. And that trouble is in the shape of a bunch of reindeer in leather jackets. The ninja tries to help out with the lights, but everybody is like, "Get out of here!" And they keep picking and picking and picking on the ninja until he can't take it anymore. So he grabs one deer by the fur and they stare at each other about ten seconds. Then the ninja kicks the reindeer's legs and hooves. The other deer start crying, which makes the ninja kick even harder, so hard that blood dribbles out the deer's nose. When he finishes, *nobody says a word*, and they don't pick on the ninja anymore that day. Then the ninja suggests that everybody wait for the fog to clear and then deliver the presents. And guess what? It works. Santa is captivated. The ninja saves Christmas, and he finds meaning in his life. And to all the elves and reindeer, Santa says, "I don't know why, but somehow someway, everyone needs a ninja in their life." And that's basically why the reindeer stop talking crap—they were scared. And, in[39] the[40] end,[41] sometimes[42] that's[43] just[44] what[45] has[46] to[47] happen.[48]

---

[39] Mom, am I important?

[40] *Of course you are!*

[41] But why, Mom?

[42] *You just are.*

[43] Yeah, but why?

[44] *Because you are!*

[45] Can't you think of anything?

[46] *What do you want me to say!*

[47] Anything!

[48] *Go to bed!*

The Future
(According to Ninjas)

Ninjas can see into the future. That's why ninjas are so good at fighting. They know when someone is about to punch them, so they can jump out of the way. Sometimes it's like slow-motion to them, and other times it's like a day-dream, but cooler. Here are some predictions of the future written by ninjas:

- Bedtimes will be outlawed and hot babes will be in-lawed (but in a good way).
- School will consist only of lunchtime, recess, and going home.
- Toys will be free—mainly the cool ones. But stupid toys can still cost money, I don't care.
- Ideals and absolute truth will be replaced by a real nice ass beating.
- Ambulances will have bunk beds in case a buddy wants to come along.
- Bunk beds will have bunk beds.
- Vegetables will be made out of ice cream.
- Boobs will be legal on TV and in public. They don't have to be huge though, but they do have to be boobs.
- So-called best friends won't just like you when they feel like it.
- "No" will be replaced with "maybe." And "maybe" will be replaced with "probably."

- You'll be able to have sex in a video game, and you[49] won't[50] have[51] to[52] be[53] an[54] adult[55] this[56] time.[57]

> **A Ninja Makes a Telephone Call**
>
> | **Whiskers:** | Meow |
> |---|---|
> | **Ninja:** | Hello. |
> | **Whiskers:** | |
> | **Ninja:** | Hello. . . . Anyone there? |
> | **Whiskers:** | Meow. |
> | **Ninja:** | I thought you left. Are we still on for Thursday? |
> | **Whiskers:** | Meow. |
> | **Ninja:** | Are you sure? |
> | **Whiskers:** | |
> | **Ninja:** | Well, whatever. Just be there. |

---

[49] Robert, this is the future you.

[50] What?

[51] Yup.

[52] Oh, wow. What's your problem?

[53] I came back to warn you.

[54] Warn me! About what?

[55] On Friday, November 15, 2014 at 2:16 P.M., you will think you have to fart. But that fart feeling is just a poop feeling in disguise. And the future you (me) pushes hard enough to let loose a cube of charcoal that rolls out of your pant leg. And guess what? Your boss sees EVERYTHING.

[56] No way!

[57] For real. So on Friday, November 15, just chill. Alright?

A Shakespearian Play: *The Choice*

Throughout history, famous musicians wrote songs about ninjas and famous writers wrote movies about them. Even fancy people, like Shakespeare, were into ninjas. Here's one of his last plays before everybody started liking him:

The Choice

ENTER MC MC INTO LIVING ROOM
Mc Mc: I am alone and, alas, I am lonely.

ENTER NINJA THROUGH WINDOW
Ninja: Fair Sir! I heard your pleas! And I've come to help and hang out.
Mc Mc: I can't believe it.
Ninja: Believe.
Mc Mc: O.K.
Ninja: So what's your problem?
Mc Mc: Everybody hates me.
Ninja: What! That's bull crap. I don't hate you.
Mc Mc: Are you joking or serious?
Ninja: Serious. Why would I hang out with you in this scene if I didn't like you?
Mc Mc: Good point.
Ninja: Thank you. Now listen. If you believe in something Totally Sweet, like ninjas or something else, then you will never ever be lonely again.
Mc Mc: But why is this so, *mon ami*?

Ninja:	If your happiness depends on buddies and they vanish, then so will your happiness, which sucks.
Mc Mc:	But why do buddies run away?
Ninja:	Humans are very scared animals. They're scared of what people will think about them when they lose themselves in something Totally Sweet.
Mc Mc:	It's like when you get pumped, people get mad at you.
Ninja:	No joke. It's so stupid. But I and my kind will always understand you, and you will understand us. And we will be together hanging out, hard, until the end of space and time, and after that, who cares?
Mc[58] Mc:[59]	Yeah,[60] who cares?

The End

---

[58] You know, Robert, I was thinking. I know you've been having trouble with your friends and parents. We're all trying to overcome that part of our lives. **—John, ed.**

[59] Wait, what?

[60] Well, you really can't stop talking about them. I don't know what to tell you about Mark, but maybe this story will help you out with your mom and dad. When I was ten, I thought my parents were rotten, too. They made me do chores and vacuum and come home before dark. I felt I had no freedom, like they were trying to control me like an animal, and I would get so mad. But something terrible happened—my parents were in a near fatal car crash. They went out to pick up some groceries at a nearby market, and a moose walked out into the street. But they drove around it. But before my parents got home, they hit a bump and, because their seat belts weren't fastened, they both popped out the sunroof. Fortunately, they lived and were only in the hospital for a short time. But for the next few weeks, I had to do my own laundry, pack my lunch, and even spank myself when I misbehaved. But, pretty soon, I started to miss having parents around, making sure I was safe and punishing me. The thing is, they understood me just about as much as I understood them. They weren't trying to control me because of some sick fetish. They were just trying to teach me and keep me safe. Do you understand what I'm saying, Robert?

A Ninja's Letter to Santa

Santa lives on the coldest place on Earth—Antarctica, because he's doesn't give a crap. I respect that. His house is full of robots and military equipment in case somebody gets the stupid idea of breaking in. Below is a ninja's letter to Santa:

Dear Santa,

I know I haven't been very good. In fact, some might even call me naughty, because of the killing and stabbing. But I think you might be the only one who understands me. I remember once when I was a young boy, I sat on your lap at the mall. (Do you remember me?) Well, you asked me what I wanted, and no one ever said that before. At the time, I couldn't think of anything. But now, I thought I could ask you for this one thing . . . I want you to beat up some people for me: Rick and Charlotte Hamburger. I can't do it, because I'm busy you know, cutting off heads and stuff. But I know you can do it—I feel it all through my body. Besides, these people haven't celebrated your birth in OVER TEN YEARS. And when I ask them about your holiness, they say you think I'm annoying or obnoxious. But I know that's not true. You know me. I only ask for this one thing. Beat them. Beat them till you fall asleep. Make it your hobby, I don't care. But remember this—I know what you're capable of, and I know we both want this. Anyways, just let me know about your answer. You can circle either yes or no and send this back to me. But don't take tooooooooo long.

YES   NO

O.K.! See ya later!

Your servant/friend,
A REAL Ninja

Santa's Reply

Santa
Manager
Christmas Town, Antarctica

Dear Ninja,

I regret to inform you that I cannot fulfill your request to beat up Mr. and Mrs. Hamburger. The applicant pool for ass-beatings this year has been very large, and there were only a few openings available. Furthermore, I might add that Rick and Charlotte are beautiful people/parents. In fact, some even believe Charlotte is an angel—she bakes! And Rick, well he's a saint. He would never hurt anyone without just cause. So, I must conclude, I will not beat up Mr. and Mrs. Hamburger. I love them.

Second, I would like to take some time to tell YOU the real truth about ninjas. Ninjas don't flip out and kill people. They are courteous and don't get all wound up on sugary treats and yell or cause trouble or embarrass their parents. They respect bedtimes *and other people*. Their purpose is to serve parents, because of their loving nature. Essentially, they should go unnoticed until they can pay their own bills and[61] buy[62] their[63] own[64] food.[65]

Santa[66]

---

[61] Is that you, Mom? Get out of here!

[62] *Look, you little shit.*

[63]

[64] *Look at me when I'm talking to you!*

[65] What.

[66] *I know you've been speaking a lot of crap about me in your book. But I don't understand why. You came directly out of my vagina—you owe me. So what's your problem? Can you please stop embarrassing your father and me? How would you like it if I were to embarrass you? How would you like it if I went to your school and started making out with your classmates? I bet you'd feel pretty stupid. And just picture me hanging out at the playground topless, or ovulating in your lunch bag. Now chill out, you little son of a bitch.*

Plato's Allegory of the Hole, Probably by Plato

SMARTICUS

Bonjour, amigo!

FAGOMONIUS

Yo, bonjour.

SMARTICUS

Did you know humans live in a big hole?

FAGOMONIUS

What!

SMARTICUS

Yup. Light gets in through the top and everybody in the hole is trapped.

FAGOMONIUS

Wow! No crap!

SMARTICUS

Vertas, my friend. Very vertas. And these people think that getting pumped is just about going to a movie or playing basketball once in a while.

FAGOMONIUS

Isn't it?

SMARTICUS

No way! These people are deceived by sit-coms. And they aren't allowed to turn their heads away from the TV, 'cause they'll get slapped in the mouth. But most importantly, they aren't able to look out and see the ninjas standing above, trying to help them.

FAGOMONIUS

Who are these ninjas?

SMARTICUS

I will tell you.

FAGOMONIUS

O.K.

SMARTICUS

Ninjas are the human form of being pumped up. And they hold ropes for the regular people to climb out. Only when somebody escapes, they can understand REAL Ultimate Power.

FAGOMONIUS

Has anyone made it out?

SMARTICUS

A few. But when they go back to teach the others, they are poo-pooed. Nobody listens and they are beaten.

FAGOMONIUS

That's so immature.

SMARTICUS

Si.

The[67] **End**[68]

---

[67] Hey Robert, that's kinda like you. You're the teacher going back into the hole, don't you think?—**John, ed.**

[68] I don't know what I am.

Famous Ninjas in History

Did You Know?

Mom said that if I didn't return my videos to the video store on time, then a motorcycle gang would come to my house and beat the crap out of me. I believe her. But she also said that if I didn't wear my dress pants to school on picture day, she'd uppercut me. I didn't believe her, but I should have.

One time Mom, Dad, and I drove to my aunt's house for Easter. And after a while, my bladder was like, "Yo!" Mom was like, "Too bad. Should have said something before we left." I was O.K. for a little while, but as soon as I couldn't hold it any longer,

Mom said, "Fifteen minutes and we're there. So shut up." I saw my eyes pass before my life and everything sucked. Muscles began to shake, my legs, everything. All that was holding back the pee were these little muscles and that's it. Imagine holding up a basketball over your head for over an hour. You couldn't do it. I thought about peeing in the car and taking whatever they gave me. But as soon as we pulled in my aunt's driveway, I busted out of the car and ran toward the pond and let loose. Later, when Dad was spanking me, I realized that most of life was BULLCRAP. I knew right then that *need* was a four-letter word. "I need a new bike." "I need to go to the mall." Yeah, right! Everything became completely clear and sweet. I made a choice to learn all about ninjas and teach others the way of REAL Ultimate Power. Everything else was[69] for[70] stupid[71] babies.[72] Here is how[73] some[74] real[75] ninjas[76] started[77] their[78] journeys[79] toward[80] Total[81] Sweetness:[82]

Quak

This ninja grew up on a farm with horses and cows and chickens. Everyday he had to feed them, even though he didn't care about them at all. But early one morning, his parents awoke to find all

---

[69] Mom, do you believe in me?

[70] *What do you mean believe in you?*

[71] You know. Do you think I could do anything I want to?

[72] *I don't think you could fly or see the future.*

[73] No, Mom! I mean like be President or something?

[74] *Doubt it.*

[75] What about Governor?

[76] *Nope.*

[77] Mayor?

[78] *How big is the town?*

[79] REALLY SMALL.

[80] *How small?*

[81] A couple people.

[82] *Maybe.*

the animals in a huge pile, burning. Quak didn't want to feed them anymore. That's when his parents knew that he was special.

Yugo

Alright, when people talk about stealth, they're usually talking about this guy. He was so sneaky nobody ever knew he was there. So . . . there's really not much to say about him.

Francis

A mother and daughter were sprinkling bread on the beach, and pigeons were flopping around all over the place. They loved each other and the pigeons knew it. But behind them, off in the distance, stood a young boy watching and screaming, because their relationship was so beautiful. When mommy and baby left, squeezing each other's hands so tight, the kid walked over to the stupid, stupid pigeons. They looked up at him and thought he had dessert but, nope, he picked up two of them and scurried over to a pipe that was spewing tar onto the beach. "I love you," he said to each pigeon as he stuffed them into the pipe, which made the pipe gurgle and squirt. "You're going home," he whispered. He then looked around and saw a bunch of people watching him, and he realized right then that he couldn't go back to the simple care-free life of school and bubbles. He would never be forgiven and would eventually suffer. And, with everything he did from then on, he left behind more and more of his former self, removing anything human from his character, until there was nothing left except one completely awesome ninja.

Tony

Tony lived in a suburb. He was captain of the basketball team *and* the soccer team—and his parents loved every minute of it. He was only a simple kid, but he had every type of toy a person could want. And when his mom took him shopping before Christmas, he would get EVERYTHING. She'd drag him around the store and push his head right into a shelf full of toys and make him nod his head toward his next present. He had all those badass toys and was sure to get more as long he did what he was supposed to. But one day, Tony came to school without his homework finished. And the teacher was like, "What happened?" And he was like, "My pencil broke," and he started walking away. But then the teacher said, "Why didn't you use a pen?" Then Tony turned around and said, "I didn't want to." And the teacher didn't say shit for the rest of the year. After that, he turned in all his homework late, then with spots on it, and eventually just the spots. Soon, making the bed became a complete joke and his parents started freaking out. They tried to get him to come back by giving him more toys, but Tony didn't speak that language anymore. When people saw him, they were scared. He was an animal. He no longer gave a crap.

Frank

One time, there were these abandoned fields that were full of ghosts. Nobody ever wanted to go through them, because they knew they would be killed. But one day, these two boys from another village decided to walk through, because of their stupidity. When the townspeople saw them go in, they were like, "Morons." And they were. They kept walking and walking and walking and nothing happened, except when they came to this gigantic hill. There, they saw a dog sitting on top of the hill. But the dog wasn't a normal dog. (I think you know what it was.) They kept walking toward the dog, and it didn't move or say anything. And pretty soon they were standing right over it, but the dog still didn't move. But when the boys looked down, they didn't see paws. They saw human hands! And the kids started shaking, hard. The dog stood up on its two back hands and strangled the slowest boy. And then the dog yelled to the other boy to stop running because he had a message for the others and the boy ran back. Then the dog was like, "Tell the others that . . ." and the dog started to strangle the other boy, too! When the boys' parents heard about it, they almost died of heart attacks. And their neighbors were depressed for over a week. It was the saddest day in the community, but not the saddest day for the dog. He didn't even care, because that damn dog was a ninja!

A Ninja Makes a Telephone Call

Guy: Hello.

Ninja: Do you want milk?

Guy: Excuse me?

Ninja: Is that it, little baby? Does the little baby want some milk, 'cause he's thirsty? Whah! Whaaaaaaaaaaaaaaaaaaaaaah!

Guy: I don't understand what you're talking about. Why are you talking to me this way?

Ninja: Oh, the little baby can't understand simple words like *milk*. What a dumb baby! You want milk so bad, but you're just too little and too dumb to do anything about it. Roll over in your baby bed and cry, you baby.

Guy: O.K., well, I'll be going now.

Ninja: Bye-bye, you stupid, stupid, baby! Whaaaaaaaaaaaah!

The Classifieds

In case you sometimes wake up at night and start to worry whether ninjas *reallllly* exist, go back to sleep. 'Cause there's a ninja out there right now who cares about you, or at least cares about killing you (which is something, I guess). Don't believe me? Then look at these classified ads in a fancy newspaper:

• Single mother of three boys seeking man for husband purposes. Needs to be old and must be willing to put up with extreme stupidity.

• Baby-sitter wanted. No experience needed, must be willing to put up with a kid who acts retarded and can't shut his mouth. Will take anybody. Please contact as soon as possible. Hurry.

• Ninja seeking pupil/son/buddy. Just wants to hang out with a kid who's cool and doesn't give a crap. Will *promise* to always be there, no matter what.

• Mad scientist seeking awesome boy to give him powers cooler than just about anything. WARNING: This is not a joke. So only apply if you really mean it. Peace out!

• Friend in need. Looking for somebody who will always pick up the phone, even if they're tired or crabby. Doesn't have to be good at anything or cool. Just has to be able to get a ride over here or can pick me up. That's all.

• Kidnapper seeking kid who is willing to move in as early as this month. Must like huge amounts of toys and must be able to sleep in really late. All applicants must be very good at [83] video [84] games, [85] otherwise [86] don't [87] bother. [88]

---

[83] MOM!

[84] *What!*

[85] Look!

[86] *What!*

[87] I'm doing the splits!

[88] *That's dumb.*

The History of Yoga

After World War II, martial arts were banned everywhere in Japan. They wanted everybody to calm down after the war. But after a while, Japanese people started to think that ninjas were pointless, which seems crazy, but it happened and it was wrong. Many gave up the ninja suit and sword in exchange for the business suit and wok. Idiots. But there were a few who practiced the art of ninjas even if they weren't allowed to take karate. These are the ones who had to be ninjas because nothing else made sense. But instead of training with karate, they used yoga. Yoga got started in Shaolin Temples. Originally, they had over eighteen moves. But that was too complicated so they shrunk it down to one move—the splits.

Before it got popular, yoga was a HUGE secret among monks. The monks taught yoga to their neighbors to defend themselves from thieves who robbed and hit them. Nobody was allowed to have weapons back then either, because the government said so. So the thieves were basically able to steal anything they wanted, no problem. The whole thing was pretty ridiculous, but fortunately yoga helped the monks when everything else failed. They found safety and comfort in the stretched hug of yoga's legs and everything became a little bit manageable. So they were able to fend off their enemies till one day, a real ninja would come[89] and[90] take[91] them[92] away.[93]

---

[89] Dude, I found this note plastered on several trees in the neighborhood. Would you happen to know anything about it?—**John, ed.**

Dear Anybody,

If you would like to kidnap me, then please go right ahead. I can vacuum and I have a dog that's awesome. I can't do back flips yet, but that doesn't mean I won't be able to in the future.

I get out of school around 3:30. You could do it then or when I take out the trash on Saturday mornings, around eight o'clock. But I go right back to bed after I take out the trash—so you probably won't see me outside till later that afternoon. Sometimes my dog and I wrestle outside on the front lawn, but we don't have a set time for that kind of stuff. You could just wait across the street in a van or black Cadillac and strike whenever. Or, you could send me a signal, maybe a note taped to the dog, that tells me where and when and then I'll make sure to be there and go limp when you start chasing me. Is that cool?

Hope to be hearing from you,
your future roommate,

Robert

[90] No way! I didn't write that. That must be the other Robert—the one down the street.

[91] But he's over fifty years old!

[92] Yeah, but he's having trouble at home.

[93] I had no idea.

Historical Letters from a Ninja Pupil

Every so often, a ninja kidnaps a kid and trains him and everything. They get to learn about ninjas and can do basically anything they want. Below is a collection of letters from the luckiest kid I've ever heard of:

JARED PLYMPTON

Classification: Non-Family Abduction
Missing: 04/26/03
From: Lake Orion, MI
Sex/Race: Male/White
DOB: 03/21/95

Eyes: Blue
Hair: Blonde
Height: 4′ 8″
Weight: 140 lbs
Identifying Marks: Front teeth protrude slightly, small scar under right eye from showing off with scissors during his younger brother's birthday party.
Jewelry: n/a
Last Seen Wearing: Red coat, green plaid shirt, and green jeans.

Evidence

Dear Mom and Dad,

Hey! Just wanted to let you know I'm O.K. A ninja takes care of me now. Can you believe it? He's pretty cool. I get my own room here and I don't have to share it with a brother or anything. Now that's pretty cool. He says you guys are mad at me, because I left a pen in my pocket and screwed up an entire load of wash. Is that true? He said that you guys don't ever want to see me again. I thought that was a little immature on your part, but sometimes I guess that's just the way things go. Oh, and guess what—I don't have to go to school here either. And I get to play video games all day! I play right when I get up and the ninja watches me from his recliner. I like it here. I don't have to make my bed or ANYTHING. Cool.

Bye!
Jar

Dear Parents,

Hi. Just telling you I'm still doing good, though I don't really get to go outside much here. I don't like that part, but I guess I can't complain because he takes me to his brother's place and I get to run around his trailer that's out in some field. He says it's for my own good, which makes sense. We eat spaghetti every night, which is AWESOME. Remember when I'd ask you to cook spaghetti, Mom, and you'd be like, "Nah, Dad doesn't like it." Well, *I like it*, and I get to eat it here all the time—so tell everybody.

Bye,
Jar

––––––––––

Dear Jane and Marvin,

I changed my name now. He said I have to, because I'm a different person now and I have to give something up to start my new life. Sorry, but I'm not supposed to tell you the new one, though. I'm getting a little sick of spaghetti. And the video games aren't that much fun anymore. Oh, remember when Dad ate a whole pizza at once that one time! That was crazy! And remember when we made that snowball fort, and I wanted to live out there for the rest of the winter, and you were like, "No way, Jose!" I was so mad at first, but now I understand. O.K., gotta go.

Bye,
Can't-tell-you

––––––––––

Dear Parents,

The ninja drove me to his brother's on Sunday again. I got to play with a dog for a few minutes. That dog barks so much! And there's a HIGHWAY near the trailer and I hear a RIVER to the EAST, but I'm not sure. And when

I we drive home, I sometimes see AIRPLANES in the sky. Big ones, like the kind that would land at AIR-PORTS. And if we ever meet again, I will never *ever* ask you to make spaghetti and I'll replace the clothes I messed up. All of them. Just give me another chance.

See ya later (please)!
Jar

Some kids are so frigg'n lucky. I HATE IT! If a ninja kidnapped me, I wouldn't write home or anything. I don't know what that kid's problem is. There's no way anybody could think that ninjas aren't sweet.[94]

---

[94] Robert, I think you've hit something very important here. What makes something totally sweet? Is it because people think it's sweet? Or is it because there's some necessary property of the ninja that makes it totally sweet? That is, ninjas are sweet regardless of what people think about them, because the characteristic of being a ninja implies being sweet. Let me define some terms first. A **necessary property** is a property an object has because it follows from another property the object is defined as having. For example, suppose I define a triangle as a three sided figure. From the property of being three sided, it follows that a triangle has the necessary property of having three corners, because if the triangle didn't have three corners, it couldn't have three connecting sides. Simple enough. Further, **a contingent property** is a property that doesn't follow from properties an object is defined as having. Taking our above definition of triangle, it doesn't follow that a triangle has to have sides of equal length, since a figure can have three sides of differing lengths and still be a triangle. O.K., now the question remains whether sweetness is a necessary or contingent property of a ninja. If it's a necessary property, then a ninja is sweet no matter what. If it's contingent, then, I hate to say it, it's possible that a ninja might not be sweet. Although ninjas don't like to be defined, we'll do so for the purposes of this argument. Let's say that a ninja is a being that flips out and kills people, wails on guitars, and porks more babes than anybody. Now we have to ask if it's possible to be flipping out and kill people, wail on guitars, and pork more babes than anybody and not be sweet. Needless to say, the answer is no. Nobody can do all that stuff and not be sweet. So sweetness is a necessary property of ninjas. So ninjas are sweet no *matter what.*—**John, ed.**

The Most Controversial Case EVER

Want to really know why ninjas are so sweet? There is this court case where a bunch of ninjas get sued by the United States of America for purging about how sweet they are. This one kid knew the judge somehow and was able to get the transcripts and everything. When I read this, I crapped my pants twice. It's awesome. Hopefully you won't/will crap your pants, too.

THE UNITED STATES OF AMERICA
vs.
A BUNCH OF NINJAS

A bunch of ninjas are sitting around a table totally pissed while some idiot judge is yelling at them for hours. They are about to be sued for trillions of dollars for purging about how sweet they are. But out of nowhere, this badass motorcycle explodes through the window. The lawyer riding it is wearing all black and is looking pretty sweet. Smoke is everywhere and everybody is screaming (except the ninjas, of course). The lawyer is like, "Everybody, chill." And the judge is like, "Order in my court!" but his hair is sticking straight up and he is now wearing dark shades. The lawyer says, "I have come to defend these *TOTALLY SWEET* ninjas right here." The judge is like, "Yo, wait, that has yet to be decided." And the lawyer is like, "Oh yeah?" And the judge is like, "Yeah." And the lawyer is like, "Let's ROCK!"

The Case for the Total Sweetness of Ninjas

Judge: Hereye, hereye!

Mr. Smooth Black: Good afternoon your honor and fellow jury members. Mr. Smooth Black for the representation of all ninjas worldwide.

Judge: What's your problem?

Mr. Smooth Black: Well, your honor, my best friends here have been accused of a bunch of BULLCRAP!

Judge: Order in the court right now, or I'll file you content. So chill, asshole!

Mr. Smooth Black: Maybe you're the real asshole. I bet you don't know anything about Total Sweetness.

Judge: Well, guess what?

Mr. Smooth Black: What?

[HUGE pause]

Judge: Maybe YOU don't know anything about Total Sweetness.

Mr. Smooth Black: YEAH RIGHT! Why don't you shut your skinny mouth and let me tell you why, item by item, these ninjas are the sweetest guys ever.

Item 1:   Ninjas kill people.

Item 2:   Ninjas don't give a crap.

Item 3:   Ninjas flip out hard.

Item 4:   Ninjas can kill people, not give a crap, and flip out hard, *at the same time*.

Item 5:   Ninjas don't even know what "bedtime" means.

Item 6:   Ninjas don't need to go to school to learn a bunch of crap that they will never use. They only need to learn "cut" and "head" and that's it.

Item 7:   Ninjas will not feel obligated to buy some shoes after having been assisted by a shoe salesman for over thirty minutes.

Item 8: Ninjas won't talk crap about you if they don't know anything about you.

Item 9: Ninjas will not buy a bunch of crap they don't need just because it's half off.

Item 10: A ninja will never break your heart—that is, *metaphorically* speaking.

Item 11: If a ninja babe owes you a blow job, you will never have to be in the awkward position of asking for it.

Item 12: A ninja will never cop a 'tude with his homies.

Item 13: A niinja will not lie to your face about some shit when you know the truth about that shit and the shit's obvious and it's obvious you know the shit.

Item 14: A ninja won't require that you make your bed when *EVERYBODY* knows that it will be messy later that night.

Item 15: A ninja won't make you do something in a less efficient manner just because "he's the boss" and "it is how it's always been done."

Item 16: If they want, ninjas can eat ice cream and tacos for breakfast, lunch, and dinner, and nobody is going to give a crap.

Item 17: Ninjas are fabulous dancers.

After the lawyer said all that stuff, the judge jumped on his desk and started wailing on a guitar. Everybody went nuts and started partying hard. The case was thrown out that very second and, apparently, the ninjas and judge still hang out every[95] once[96] in[97] a[98] while.[99]

---

[95] *Robert, go to bed RIGHT NOW!*

[96] O.K., Mom.

[97] *What was that?*

[98]

[99] *Yeah, that's what I thought! You know it's not too late to send you to an orphanage, with that attitude you've got. And I'll do it, too. Watch me. You just be thankful that you've got a roof over your head and parents that tolerate you very much.*

Intermission
(Snack Break/Mini-Pump)

Now it's time to take a short little break from the regular hustle and bustle of homework and dogs and stuff, and reflect on your life AND get pumped up. The following script is about a ninja accepting his past and killing people.

Tear Drop

The scene opens with a car slamming down the street. Sparks and smoke are flying everywhere and the wheels are covered with blood. (This will give the audience a clue to who's driving it.) The camera will spin around the car and look right at its license plate which says "Death." This will foreshadow what's gonna happen to some idiot-cry-babies later. As the car speeds down the street, flames are coming out of the pipes and people are so scared—they can't protect themselves, and they are little wimps. Fortunately for nobody, the driver is a ninja. And he's slamming the gas so hard his foot busts the frigg'n floor out of the car, which bounces off the street and hits a family right in the face. Headlines of the family's death and stupidity will be on news-papers flying toward the camera for suspense. As the car rips out chunks of the street, a poor little orphan is standing on some garbage for height and puts his thumb up to "hitchhike." The ninja sees the poor baby, just standing there like a frigg'n wimp-jerk. And the ninja stops the car, smirks, bites the kid's thumb off, and puts it in a plastic bag in the back seat. Several people see the travesty and start running from the road. They'll be running like retards to make the audience laugh even harder. Then the ninja sees the orphanage where the kid came from. He's pissed. The place is so full of little dummies that the walls are bending. The camera will watch from behind as the ninja's car smashes and explodes right toward the flimsy building. But out of nowhere, the ninja SLAMS on the breaks. And a little baby boy crawls right in front of the car. That's when the ninja will remember his past. Then the ninja approaches the baby, lifts him up, and stuffs him in his mouth like a crazy bird. As the baby goes down his throat, the audience will feel uncomfortable, but they will later hear the ninja screaming, and it's actually the baby inside and then they'll laugh! As the ninja drives right into the orphanage, while screaming with a tiny baby voice, the camera will zoom right into the ninja's eye to see a little tear drop. Then the orphanage EXPLODES, and the orphans fly toward the camera, completely smothering it.

The End

That's enough, I'm[100] soaked.[101]

---

[100] I was thinking, Robert, doesn't being pumped all the time make you tired?—**John, ed.**

[101] I have to sleep once in a while, but when I do, I do it hard. I *slam* my head into the pillow.

PART III

Ninjas Everyday

A poor peasant man bumped into a lady getting water from a well. They talked and hung out. The peasant loved the woman so much, but she didn't even care. And HE DID EVERYTHING FOR HER. Before the peasant left for the city, he asked the poor woman to join him. The woman was like, "Nope." Then the peasant began to walk away, but he stopped, thought for a moment, then turned around and scratched her eyes out.

—Ancient Chinese Fable

Many people think that ninjas don't exist because they never see them. But ninjas are everywhere. Like this one time a ninja was hiding in my aunt's salad, and she didn't even know it. And another time, this old lady was peeling an orange and thought it was regular fruit. But no. Sparks started coming out of the peel and it exploded. Her face was covered with juice and she kept yelling for help, but nobody wanted to deal with her at that moment.

In this section, I am going to teach you how to relate to ninjas in your daily life by showing you how to spot one, how to decipher their desires, and how they affect people like me. Plus, we're going to get a little more personal and talk about their fantasies and fears so we can relate to them on even deeper levels. I'm going to show you that ninjas are similar to regular people, and that just about anybody could be one.

Personally, I haven't actually seen a ninja, but one time, Francine and I went to find one in our neighborhood. We woke up super early and Francine was so tired that I had to sprinkle water on her eyes to get her to sit up. After getting dressed, we slid down the stairs and spread our legs and arms to avoid making any squeaking noises commonly associated with feet. Then we squeezed through the dog door and I got all covered with fur, which helped me blend into nature. We looked for the first clue, but for the first five minutes I wanted to give up sooooo bad, because no one was even outside yet. But we didn't. (That's called passion, if you didn't already know). We walked down the street until we saw a couple of candy wrappers. I thought we were getting closer. Then we looked inside Mr. Felt's window. He and his wife were getting up for work and everything. I guess Mr. Felt couldn't find his glasses. He flipped over the mattress and started screaming at his wife, which made Francine nauseous. He kept pointing at her and she just stood there, nodding her head. Francine and I were so scared, but we stayed and watched anyway. Even though we didn't find any ninjas that day, they are no joke—ninjas are out there and they're making a difference.

Spotting Ninjas and the REAL Ultimate Ninja Test

Did You Know?
Most ninjas are born with pubic hair, unless they opt otherwise.

Regular people don't know the first or second thing about spotting ninjas. Just wearing black and owning a couple ninja stars doesn't mean someone is a ninja—there's a lot more to it. Fortunately for you, I am going to tell you what to look for, because you never know—a friend, enemy, or even a relative[102] might[103] be[104] one.[105] Here are some signs that somebody is a ninja, as well as the REAL Ultimate Test:

Signs That Someone Is a Ninja

First, look for the most obvious signs of ninja behavior—someone making fists without even knowing it, popping boners, making forts out of cushions and blankets, throwing dirt chunks, and running around the living room *nonstop*. If you see any of this crap, there's an awesome chance that they're a ninja. Or, if the suspect is really pissed at someone and instead of saying, "Dude, I'm gonna beat your ass or kill you!" your suspect just plays it cool, and looks out the window, but then, the next day, the other guy winds up missing. That's another clue.

But there are some other, more intimate signs that aren't as obvious. People who are ninjas are pretty much normal on the

---

[102] Though, not just *any* relative could be one. There's no way moms are ninjas.

[103] Yeah, a lot of people get that confused. Some are inclined to believe that moms may be ninjas, but this belief is obviously false when we consider the properties of moms and ninjas. If a mom is a ninja, then a mom is numerically identical to a ninja—that is, they are one and the same object. Two objects are numerically identical if and only if they have all the same properties (intrinsic and relational). Intrinsic properties are properties an object has in and of itself, *not* in relation to other objects—having a particular genetic makeup is an intrinsic property. Relational properties are properties that an object has in relation to other objects—having cut off Billy's head is a relational property. Suppose that moms and ninjas are numerically identical. Now, let's look at the properties of moms and ninjas. Both ninjas and moms scream a lot—so they both have the property of screaming. But, moms will always try to stop you from flipping out, while ninjas get pissed when you don't. So, ninjas have the property of wanting you to flip out, while moms don't. But, if moms and ninjas were numerically identical, then moms and ninjas would have all the same properties. But, as we can see above, ninjas have a property that moms don't have. So moms and ninjas don't have all the same properties. So, moms and ninjas aren't numerically identical! So, a mom cannot be a ninja.—**John, ed.**

[104] What a relief. Thanks, John. I thought that was true, but I didn't know how to express it. Now I feel pumped *and* peaceful.

[105] No problem, homey.

outside. They eat and sleep and watch TV, just like you and me, but there's just something that makes them sweeter. Here's the main stuff to watch out for:

Not Good at Reading

A lot of ninjas aren't that great at reading and don't even know why 'cause it's not their fault and they're trying really hard. It's also pretty common that other people in their family don't read very well either. Plus, they have trouble working with numbers and spelling. A ninja constantly confuses left from right and they try not to read in front of others at all costs. Once, there was this teacher who asked this kid, I don't know who he was, to read some practice sentences out loud and the kid just lay there on his desk. A classmate slapped his shoulder, but the kid didn't even move. Needless to say, the kid slept through all of read-sentences-out-loud-week and had a dream where he was principal of the entire school and he made love to all the teachers while the kids were napping and, surprisingly, the teachers were amazing.

Easily Distracted

People who are easily distracted are probably ninjas. For example, if you're talking to a ninja and people are shooting basketballs in the background, then you can forget it, because he won't hear a thing you say.

Hyperactive

They keep moving their feet, pulling girls' hair for no reason, talking during class time, and constantly interfering with the other children's learning.

Impulsiveness

If a ninja sees a donut, it will probably end up in his mouth and on his shirt. Ninjas don't think twice about anything, especially stuff like Christmas lists and sacrifice. They don't mess around with questioning themselves or their sexuality—if they like a girl, they just ask them to make out, no problem. If they want to do the splits,[106] they[107] just[108] do[109] it,[110] even if they're in line for a movie. They just don't give a crap—I'm serious. Now, look around your neighborhood for people who just can't stop. Maybe try offering people potato chips and watch how many they take. Then you'll know for sure.

Other than that, you've got to watch out for a person who:

- Has trouble paying attention to details or makes careless mistakes in schoolwork or other activities, because who cares when Thomas Jefferson did all that crap? What's important is that it happened and it was cool.
- Blurts out answers before hearing the full question, because he already knows the question and it's completely stupid to wait if the entire point is to give the answer.
- Has difficultly waiting in line or for a turn because other people aren't moving fast enough.
- Has problems with interrupting or intruding, because people are always saying a bunch of bullcrap they know nothing about.

However, the only *real* way to tell if someone is a ninja is to give them the REAL Ultimate Test. Follow these instructions and you'll know for sure.

---

[106] You know what would be badass?—**John, ed.**

[107] What?

[108] Somebody driving a car while they're doing the splits. They'd have each leg hanging out a window and their torso sticking out the sunroof.

[109] Dude! That would be so sweet. But how are they going to hit the gas?

[110] Levers, duh!

The REAL Ultimate Test

1. Get a baby carrot from the crispy drawer. (You don't need anything bigger.)
2. Put the carrot in the freezer until it's completely freezing cold.
3. Wait for your suspect to bend over, like when they're getting something from the fridge.
4. Slide the baby carrot into the suspect's o-ring.
5. Wait and watch.

If the suspect is like, "What the fuck is wrong with you, you little son of a bitch! Get the fuck away from me! Why don't you act like a normal kid and play outside and get me a fucking beer! Your mother and I should have left you at the hospital, you crazy fuck," then your suspect might *not* be a ninja. But if your suspect is like, "Yo, that's not cool," or just, "No way, homey!" then you've definitely got a ninja on your hands.

Super Powers

Another thing to look for in a ninja is super powers. Ninjas can do a lot of things regular people can't, like riding a bike without a helmet. Personally, I don't like helmets, but I used to have a friend who had a basketball hoop fall on his head. The doctor said that he would have lived if he was wearing a helmet, but his body would have been all twisted up. So I'm for helmets. Below, some real ninjas tell how they discovered their super power:

William (Bill)

Ninja for four weeks

My neighbor has a brown dog. It's HUGE. One time, I was mowing the lawn and the dog just started running at me, but it couldn't get me because of the fence. I turned off the mower and stared at the dog. Sweat popped out of my hair and I didn't even blink. The dog didn't say a word, and then it ran back toward the neighbor's house and busted through the screen door and the people inside started squealing really hard. I knew right then that I had the power to control most brown dogs. After that, I would search for them everywhere. And when I found one, I would stare at it for as long as it took. Then they'd go FRIGG'N NUTS. They'd start spitting and rolling around the yard. And I would jump back on my bike screaming and laughing 'cause nobody would even know what happened. Dog owners would run out of their homes almost crying because their pets were so rambunctious. Their feelings of rest and relaxation from controlling their pets were lost in an explosion of chew toys and screen doors. Their lives were all changed for the better/worse because of <u>me</u>.

Darlene

Ninja for two weeks

My parents are divorced and Mom cooks brownies all the time to make up for it. But one night, she cooked a big batch because Dad came over earlier when she wasn't home and took two lamps that were actually hers. Mom set the brownies on top of the oven and said I couldn't eat ANY for at least *ten minutes*. They were hot enough to burn an adult, she said. But as soon she left, I grabbed one and stuffed it in my face. But my tongue didn't burn! That's when I knew I had the power to eat super-hot food. Later that night, I went to bed without any argument and I couldn't stop kicking my feet and snorting, thinking about all the ways I could use this badass power.

Ted

Ninja for one month

Dad got me this new alarm clock so he doesn't have to deal with me in the morning. He says he doesn't want to go to work angry—I understand where he's coming from. I was so excited that I set up the clock in my room to practice before Sunday night. I plugged the clock in and turned it over and there was this weird button on the back. I pressed it and the clock went crazy. The numbers started going lower and my hair was blown backwards. Then I looked at the clock and it read that it was twenty-three minutes ago. And I realized, right then, that I had the power to time travel. I experimented a little bit, even went back in time a couple minutes, but that got boring. So I put on a sweater and got ready to go into the future. But as I was holding in the button to go forward, I looked down, and saw a little wrinkle form on my knuckle. So I slammed the back button real quick, because I knew I wasn't ready for pubes or menopause or anything like that.

Imagine if regular people had the power[111] ninjas[112] have.[113]

---

[111] Dude, check out what I found on the kitchen counter!—**John, Ed.**

[112] What is it?

[113]   Dear Mr. and Mrs. Hamburger,

Notes to parents are rarely welcome and I'm sorry to say that this one is no different. We often make mistakes in our lives we'd rather not take credit for, like my taking this job and, I suspect, you having Robert.

During class discussion, your son Robert has consistently produced an erection, preventing the other children from learning, and I will not have that in my school. Furthermore, he has encouraged the popular kids (who are awesome) to tease him regularly. And it's hard enough trying to run a school without kids screaming and yelling cuss words all day.

At times like these, it's comforting to know that our children have some understanding of right and wrong. Robert is missing this quality. So, I am asking your permission to spank your son at school, maybe between classes or during lunch time, depending on how my day is going. I don't know if that's permitted in your home and, if it's not, maybe it's time to come over to our side. Kids Robert's age need to know that bad behavior will result in painful spankings, just like in real life. How are you supposed to explain to these kids that they shouldn't do something wrong, harmful, or disrespectful, when they don't even understand that they can't survive in space without a helmet or that an erection isn't made from real bone? Now, if you would like to talk in person about spanking techniques and bedtimes, feel free to give my secretary a call and set up an appointment. If you could get back to me as soon as possible, I would greatly appreciate it.

Thank you,
Dr. Shram, Ph.D.

And look, here's the reply letter!

Dear Dr. Shram,

You cannot imagine the embarrassment I endure when Robert "loses it" in front of people who don't know Rick and me. I want to

Now, stop.[114] Now,[115] continue[116] thinking[117] about[118] how[119] sweet[120] ninjas[121] are.[122]

---

tell them it's not our fault and that we have perfectly nice lives when he's not around. For example, I got a new job and I'm doing great. A lot of parents complain that their child has trouble in school or is hyperactive. I'd give anything for a kid who was just hyperactive. So, we don't care what you do. We are so proud to have you in our school district. Let us know if you need any help at school, too. Maybe Rick and I could chaperon some event— anything where we can yell at people. We'll do what it takes to make this community a nice, normal place.

Yours,
Rick and Charlotte

[114] IT'S A FRIGG'N CONSPIRACY!

[115] Dude, what are we gonna do?

[116] Dude, I don't know!

[116] Let's change the letter.

[117] Dude, can we do that?

[119] Why not? You dictate what you want me to write. O.K.?

[120] O.K.

Dear Principal,

What's your problem? Robert's cool. So get a life and don't bother me with this trivial crap. You DON'T have permission to spank Robert, because he's above that. Oh, and, by the way, have you ever tried to shut-up? If not, you should try it sometime—I hear it works.

Au revoir,
Robert's parents, both of them

P.S. Don't mail letters here anymore, because if you do, we'll kill you.

[121] Dude, we can't send that!

[122] FRIGG'N SEND IT—IT'S AWESOME!

Ninja Fantasies

Even though ninjas have all these powers that most people don't, they're a lot like regular people, too. They have fantasies just like you and me! Don't believe me? Then check out these fantasies, told by ninjas themselves:

Ninja Fantasy One

I'd be just sitting in school and the teacher would be like, "Learn this stuff, NOW." But as she would point back at the chalkboard, there'd be some rumbling and shaking. Bricks would fall all over the place and a crazy spider monster would bust through the wall. The spider monster would look at everybody in the class and the kids would be screaming and hiding behind tables in the back of the room, except me. I'd still be sitting at my desk, trying to ignore all the commotion and finish my homework. Then the monster would pick me out of all those kids and say, "YOU," and point right at me, "YOU ARE THE CHOSEN ONE!" And all the kids would be like, "Who is that guy?" Then I would look annoyed and start to float, and then I'd fly out the window, making the monster chase me and I'd save EVERYONE. Then, the next day, I'd come back to school, acting like nothing happened, and go to class, but I'd have a huge scar on my leg. And they'd be like, "Dude, who are you? What happened to your leg?" And I'd just look over at the girls and wink.

Ninja Fantasy Two

I'd be on this soccer team that's losing. And everybody is laughing their asses off about how bad we are. I tell my team not to worry, because I've got something pretty sweet planned, and they'd say, "Dude, you gotta help us out. If we lose this game, we're dead." And then ten minutes before recess is over, I'd pull out this remote control from my backpack and press a button. Then a futuristic car would float down from the sky, and a robot in soccer shorts would jump out right before the car landed on several assholes. The robot would run onto the field and start playing, hard. It would shoot the ball from one goal post all the way into the enemy's goal. Everybody's mouths would drop open, except mine, because the robot belonged to me. Needless to say, we would win the game easily—by about a trillion-billion points. Everybody outside would run on the field to ask me questions, but I'd just be looking over at the robot and it would be looking at me. Then I'd push all the kids aside. And we would walk toward each other, slowly. Then, as the robot picked me up and held me in its arms, I'd look at the girls and wink.

Ninja Fantasy Three

I'd just be sitting out at the bus stop, and out of nowhere this black Cadillac would pull up and a super old man would have some toys in the back seat. "Your mother told me to give you a ride to school!" he'd say. So I would crawl in back seat, and he'd take me to a secret laboratory near the Earth's core where he would give me the power to spit acid. Then he would drop me off at school and I'd say, "Thanks for the ride to school!" And we'd both laugh for a couple minutes. Then I'd slam the door, hard. And everybody would think that I got dropped off and none of that other stuff happened. Then, during lunchtime, a fire would break loose and kids would be running around, burning. I would then scream to all the lunch kids, "Yo, let's go!" and everybody would follow to me to the gymnasium. But then, a bunch of bricks would fall near the exit and some kid would say, "Nice going." But I would pretend I didn't hear him. And then the girls would start screaming hard and I'd let them keep doing it for a little while, 'cause I'd like it at first. But after a couple minutes I'd be like, "Ladies, chill. I'll get us out, today." Then I would turn around and start spitting acid all over the wall near the basketball hoops and it would crumble, because of chemistry. Then the girls would get on my back and I'd run out of the building, saving them. And then I'd drag them back behind the soccer field and make love to them as the firemen rescued the rest of the kids.

A Ninja Makes a Telephone Call

Hot Babe:	Hello.
Ninja:	Hey.
Hot Babe:	Oh, yeah.
Ninja:	Yeah?
Hot Babe:	Yeah.
Ninja:	You wanna?
Hot Babe:	Uh-huh.
Ninja:	Sweet.

The Ninja's Biggest Weakness: Super-Scary Ghost Stories

Not only do ninjas have fantasies like you and me, they also get afraid, which is O.K., because sometimes they can't help it. Their biggest weakness is super-scary ghost stories. And since my book is all about ninjas—the good and the bad—I must now give a few accounts of the ninjas' most corpulent fear. I'm sorry. The first ghost story is about a strange noise. The second is about ghost monsters and what to make of them. And the third is about a UFO, a keg of beer, and a group of very mature hippos.

The Gurgle

Apparently, there was this ninja who was hanging out with some kid. They played basketball and ate dinner together. One day the kid was like, "Do you want to hear something that will mess up your life?"

The ninja was like, "What are you talking about?"

"A real live ghost story," said the kid.

"O.K.," said the ninja.

Then the kid began, "These two buddies were eating tacos together one night at a bar and it was raining really hard outside. They were just talking. Then all of a sudden, there was a noise, like a gurgle or squirt. The buddies were like, 'What the heck is that?' And guess what . . . it happened again! They were both completely freaked out. One buddy couldn't even finish his meal. They briefly looked around the bar for clues, but they never found out what it was. And both buddies went home scared to death."

After hearing the ghost story, the ninja was so scared that he grabbed the kid and spanked him until both parties squirted urine.

The Playaz

In some other state, there were some basketball players hanging out in the forest after a big game. One player said, "This forest reminds me of some scary stuff I heard." And the other said, "What happened?" And he said, "Well, these two buddies, like you and I, were hanging out, just like now, and out of nowhere they heard something. But since they were big, like you and me, they didn't get scared. Apparently, the noise was coming from behind an old door. Together, with their hands intertwined, the buddies slowly opened the door. Then BOOM! There was a grown up standing RIGHT THERE. Then it turned around and talked. But the buddies couldn't understand a thing it said, because it had the voice of a teeny tiny baby! 'Holy crap!' said one buddy. 'Frigg'n run!' And they did."

After hearing the story, one basketball player said, "Wow!" Needless to say, a ninja over-heard the entire thing and got pretty scared/mad. The ninja didn't understand the feelings inside him and went berserk. (This is common for ninjas.) In conclusion, the players were speechless when they got their asses beat.

Le Big Party

In some cave chalk full of hippos, there was this ninja. All the hippos gathered for a ghost story. The ninja began with a warning, "If any hippo here cannot handle this type of crap, I suggest you leave right now." And some actually did. Then the ninja began. "Alright, listen. These kids were just goofing around once on the playground: sports and talking and stuff. Nobody wanted any trouble, even the bullies. Well, there was this crackle and everybody looked up. Something shiny. Then this UFO flopped on the soccer field. One kid was like, What the heck? And then its side door busted open, and fog creamed out. The assistant principle freaked out and tripped, spilling his guts on a picnic table. Nobody knew anything about anything. Then there was this rolling sound that got louder and louder and quieter and finally louder. Out of the UFO popped this giant can. It rolled past the soccer field and hit a pole. By the time the kids realized it was a keg of beer, the UFO zapped into space. Well, guess what, somebody brought a radio and turned it on loud. Then one kid grabbed Dixie cups from her duffel bag. Everybody went bananas in a good way and partied, hard. Little was understood that day, but, boy, did those kids party."

The ninja, having scared himself, beat his own ass in a paradoxical way. It was quite confusing for the hippos. But they were mature—they didn't try to make sense out of nonsense. The hippos moved on, accepting those things they could not change and surrounding themselves with only positive energy. By not defining what happened that day or their relation to it, they never limited their understanding, and they never limited themselves.

A Sensitive Ninja's Journal

> **Did You Know?**
> Even though ninjas can be emotionally unstable,
> they're still able to pursue happy, meaningful lives.

Let's start talking directly about ninjas and look at a journal written by a real one. Apparently, sensitive ninjas keep journals, which makes sense. I got the following entries from some museum, but I forgot which one. Nevertheless, we finally have some evidence of[123] their[124] inner[125] feelings[126] and[127] stuff.[128]

---

[123] Man, how much can one person talk about ninjas? I still can't believe that after all this time, you're still into them.—**John, ed.**

[124] Well, they're awesome!

[125] Yeah, yeah. I know. And I know your parents suck, too. But, I can't help thinking that your obsession is causing at least *some* of your problems. Listen, I used to work at a telemarketing company once, and there was a guy there who was obsessed with bees. He'd always read magazines about honey during his breaks. And he'd talk to the other co-workers about their experiences with bees and stinging. But the problem was that he was just *too into them*. When he

Dear anybody who reads my crap,

I'll kill you. No joke.

—A REAL ninja

Wednesday

Dear Diary,

You're the only one I can share my coolest thoughts with. Nobody I know understands Total Sweetness—so I can never reveal myself. Everybody thinks that I'm a crazy maniac killer/pimp, but deep in my catacombs, I'm really sensitive about hot babes. I like animals. When people call me names, I feel emotions. I'm a good listener. And I want my buddies to be happy, even though they don't care about my feelings sometimes. There is a bunch of love inside me, but I can only express it through cutting off heads. People just don't understand the pressure that pressures me—it's depressing. I'm a mammal without a cause! I'm a self-caused-hot-babe-lover that everybody fears for no reason except that I'll beat their ass. I'm really that simple. And nobody will take the time to listen. But I'll listen to them, and they'll talk all damn day. They never ask me any questions. And I have so much to say about snowballs, forts, spaceships, and stuff like that. It's pretty lonely being a ninja. Getting so

---

would call people to market a product, he would just end up asking them to look in their backyard and see if there were hives back there. Then, he'd start sweating when they described what they saw. So, the boss got pretty annoyed. And after a while, nobody wanted to talk to him, because he was just too weird. His problem was that he didn't try to adjust himself to the world.

[126] But why couldn't the world adjust to him?

[127] Man, I don't know. It's not that easy. You're a cool kid and I don't want you to be *that guy* when you grow up.

[128] I guess you're right. Bees are pretty retarded.

pumped all the time can be a real turnoff for friends or babes. It's like they've never been excited about anything. I'll be flipping out, and someone will be like, "Who invited that guy?" And I'll be like, "Why does it matter?" And they'll be like, "Well, I just wanted to know for personal reasons." And I'll be like, "Yeah, right." Can you believe it? Sometimes I just feel like giving up and following rules like a regular human. But you know what? That's a bunch of BULLCRAP! I'm a ninja! And my purpose is to flip out and kill people. So fuck you, diary! I'll beat your ass, too!

Thursday

In Japanese, *Mizu no Kokoro* means "a mind like water," which means that everyone should keep his mind still and calm, like a lonely pond. O.K., that sounds nice, but what if somebody throws a giant rock in the pond and the water goes nuts and the fish start screaming? Then what? I tried to find myself today. It all started earlier today when I killed this guy. I walked up behind him and cut his head off, but I didn't look at his face. Then I thought I might have killed the wrong guy, and I got super scared. I tried to set the head back on, but it kept sliding off. After a couple minutes, it finally stayed, but it still looked weird. I thought, *why do I do this to myself? Do I really need this in my life? Wouldn't it be nice to get a normal job like everybody else and have a bunch of friends who like me because I'm nice?* I could go to plays and act courteous and talk about the news, and I would try to make people feel comfortable by not killing them. And after eighty years, all these friends would be at my deathbed staring at me, and I'd stare right back and I'd think about all the work it took to make them like me. Then someone would ask, "What's your dying wish, mon ami?" And then I'd whisper something real quiet.

Everybody would look at each other and then bend down closer to hear. Then, right when they were all in place, I'd say "I love . . ." and I'd reach my hands around them and start raking my teeth across their faces, and I'd be laughing and laughing. Then I'd die in peace. I'm not a bad person, though. It's just that people don't think I have any boundaries, but I actually have a lot. I just don't brag about it every chance I get. I keep a lot of stuff inside, but I always find more room. It's like my heart is hollow like a basketball, minus the air. Maybe someday I'll be able to find someone like me.

Friday

Dear Diary,

I'm supposed to kill somebody today, but I think I'll just sleep in. Afternoon comes and I'm still a little drowsy, but I get up anyway. I look out the window and wonder about regular kids, what they're doing, if they know about people like me. I hope so. Sometimes, I pretend that I have a son that I can hang out with—you know, like buddies. If I had a real son, we could spend family time together killing people in the park, as we hold hands, together, like father and son. Then we could go to the arcade, and I could give him all the quarters I stole from mall wishing wells. And after that, we'd run through parks with masks on, hitting people and flipping over picnic tables, and later we'd watch R-rated movies and play video games and cuss ALL NIGHT LONG. Whatever HE wants! We'd kill anybody that even looked at us. And I could teach him all my tricks and secrets. And . . . one day he will grow up to kill people on his own and be a real ninja, like his father. I love you so much, mystery son, wherever you are.

How Ninjas Learn: Senseis and Training Camps

> **Did You Know?**
> You might be thinking in your heart that you don't
> understand what's going on. Well . . . neither do I.
> Maybe that comforts you. Maybe it doesn't.

I think you already know that ninjas don't go to school. I don't know how anybody in their right mind goes to school. If the president said that nobody had to go to school anymore, I can't think of one person that would be sad. NOT ONE. Except, maybe the teachers, but that's because they don't have anything else. They just yell at kids all day and go home and go to bed and that's it. One time, I saw my teacher at the grocery store. She walked right past me and kept looking straight ahead. Fortunately, ninjas don't have to deal with any of that stuff. They learn everything they know from senseis and training camps.

Senseis!

Every ninja has a sensei. A sensei is basically a ninja's teacher, but in a good way. Most of them live in dojos, but it's not a necessity. Their main job is to train ninjas to do everything—from shaving to breaking necks. There is this one sensei. *He is amazing.* Like when you say something, his eyebrows jump up and he even turns his head toward you! Unfortunately, his pupil—a spoiled idiot—never appreciated the little things the sensei did for him. For his pupil's fourteenth birthday, the sensei gave him a huge party. He even had Gloria Estefan's make-up artist, Janet, come and give everybody fake tattoos, which was awesome! I got one of a Chinese symbol that said "Hello!" But this one kid, Trey, said that symbol really meant "faggot." I don't know why Janet would do that if she *didn't even know me*. Besides, Trey's NEVER allowed to watch TV, and when the sensei put the TV in the backyard, because Mark wanted movies during his party, Trey went nuts! He just kept staring at it and everything. And when one kid started talking loud, Trey put him in a headlock and told him to be quiet in a super-weird voice. Most everybody freaked out, and half the kids called their moms to go home. I didn't leave, though, because the sensei was trying to keep the party going with dance and drink. But the important thing was that after the party, the sensei asked Mark if he got everything he wanted for his birthday. And he said, "Nah . . . I didn't like it. No turkey sandwiches." I saw the sensei's eyes get all wet, but they didn't drip. I couldn't stand it, and I ran back behind the sensei's shed and crumpled up my shirt and cried inside it. The sensei only wanted to make his pupil happy. That's all. But no. The pupil didn't even care, 'cause he didn't know what it's like in other dojos, where nobody's ever heard of fake tattoos or birthday presents or hugs or even Gloria Estefan's make-up artist,[129] Janet.[130]

Training Camps

Even though senseis teach their pupils a boatload of information, they don't learn *everything* from them. And for some ninjas who don't even have a sober sensei, there's got to be some place where they learn the basics. That's why there's summer camp. The first day is basically for getting to know everybody else—where they're from, their favorite animals and stuff. Then everybody plays volleyball, HARD! After that, they learn stuff, like hiding, sneaking around, and stealing girls' underwear—the basics. Then if they get caught 'cause it was ONLY THEIR FIRST TIME and

---

[129] "No turkey sandwiches?" Fuck that kid. He needs to get his ass beat.
—John, ed.

[130] How do you understand so much, John?

nobody's perfect at sneaking around, they make the ninja take a mental test to measure their psychic energies. You have to fit these different shaped blocks into different holes. A regular person fits the circle block into the circle hole and the square into the square. But a real ninja—I mean, a really real one—doesn't mess around with that crap. A real ninja slams the block into whatever damn hole they want. And if you pass the test, you have what it takes, and they immediately take you out of the camp. And, congratulations, you've made it to level eight, which is pretty high, if you ask anybody.

A Ninja Makes a Telephone Call

Guy: Hello?

Ninja: Get ready.

Guy: Get ready for what?

Ninja: Get ready to get your ass beat! That's what.

Guy: Are you serious, man? Why? What did I do?

Ninja: You can't shut your frigg'n mouth, always talking about people you know nothing about.

Guy: Dude, I'm sorry.

Ninja: No.

Guy: Come on, man.

Ninja: No.

Guy: I was just messing around!

Ninja: You're dead.

Guy: COME ON!

Ninja: Dude, I was just kidding.

Guy: Really?

Ninja: No.

Testimonials About Ninjas by Like-Minded Kids

Now that you've learned about the inner lives of ninjas, it's time to see what other people think about them. Ninjas aren't as bad as one may think—they don't kill *everyone* they meet. There are lots of people in my neighborhood who have been touched by a ninja (not touched like how a scout leader touches, but *changed*). Below, these real kids have real stories to tell, which can help you understand how Total Sweetness can make a difference in someone's life.

Name: Peter
Age: 11

Mr. Frez, my math teacher, is always getting mad at me because I don't get it. One time, in class, I went up to his desk to ask a question. He got so pissed. He looked around to see if anyone was watching, and then WHAM! he head-bunt me. I started to scream and everybody looked up. And Mr. Frez was like, "Don't worry, Peter, we can work out this math problem *together*." Then everybody went back to work. He helped me with the problem and he kept looking at me, smiling like he didn't do anything. I felt all fucked up inside for the rest of the day. Well, guess what, some sweet ass ninja was peeking through the window and saw the whole thing. And when Mr. Frez was driving home later that day, his car stalled—apparently *somebody* put ninja stars in his gas tank. When he got out to snoop around, there was a ninja standing right there. Mr. Frez was like, "Hey, could you help me?" Then the ninja head-bunt him so hard that Mr. Frez fell on his back and wiggled around. And the ninja didn't stop. He kept doing it until there was nothing left except blood/air. I love ninjas.

Name: Fredrick
Age: 14½

I was playing in my closet when I found my alien mask from Halloween. I put it on and went to scare Gramma who was knitting. She got so afraid that she pricked her thumb with a needle. Because she doesn't know how to express her anger well, Gramma pinched my stomach really hard. Well, you wouldn't believe it but some special friends saw her inappropriate act. Later that night, two ninjas dragged Miss-I-can't-keep-my-hands-to-myself-'cause-I'm-a-frigg'n-moron-who-uses-guilt-to-manipulate-people out to the garage and put her head in the vice on Dad's workbench. One ninja cranked the vice while the other ninja plugged her nose. I woke up from the enormous explosion and then I laughed my frigg'n ass off.

Name: Zachary
Age: 12

My dad. He's irregular, but not in a fiber way. You see, he's not like a TV dad—TV dads don't go nuts when you sneeze while they're sleeping or break your toys when you accidentally open a window. TV dads make sense. My dad makes stomachs hurt. For example, Dad would always make me bring him beer. Even when

I was really young. He'd say, "Get me another." And I would run inside and grab one, but I would go around to the driveway and grab a handful of dirt and pour it into the bottle. I would then run back into the house and out the front door to where he was sunbathing. Then I'd watch from the kitchen window as he'd spit up the dirty beer all over his hairy chest. But I didn't laugh—I just watched. And he would scream and swear. Even after he would spank me, I would still keep doing it. He kept asking me to get him a beer when he knew I was going to put dirt in it. And I knew he was going to spank me for putting dirt in, but I'd still do it. That was our relationship. But one morning while eating breakfast, I dropped a spoon on the floor when my aunts were over and he got really embarrassed. He grabbed my hair and held me over the stairway. But as he was about to drop me, there was a whistle or a quack. And there, behind him, was a ninja. The ninja's anger was huge, boiling. Nobody wished they were my dad that day, because what happened next is untellable: He grabbed my dad and tied all of his limbs in knots and made him eat four pure peanut butter sandwiches in a row. Then Dad started screaming like a[131] fat[132] dog.[133] It[134] was[135] electrifying.[136]

Dear Robert,

In reply to your letters, I'm sorry to inform you that *Diane's House of Yoga* **will not** be admitting you into our school. This is not, as your mother might think, a baby-sitting service. DHY is a serious school in the spiritual, mental, existential, philosophical, and physical art of yoga. And, trust me, it is an art.

---

[131] *Delivery! I've got a letter here for Mr. Robert Hamburger. Is that you, little man?*

[132] Uh-huh.

[133] *Hey, what are you playing there? Is that Nintendo?*

[134] Yeah.

[135] *What games you got?*

[136] Dude, get out of here.

Furthermore, yoga is not about killing people. We don't "stretch the hell out of our opponents." Yoga is about building inner strength, but more importantly—inner peace. Killing is *not* in our curriculum. Life means a lot to us here: we would prefer to better the lives of others rather than diminish them. That's why our motto is "Mo Yoga, Mo Life." You see, I take yoga very seriously. So, you can understand why I don't take kindly to those who would misuse its techniques to harm any form of life, whether it be plant, animal, or parent. The goodness of Earth's life force is within you, Robert. Even though it's misdirected, I can tell by your passion that you have real power. But you just need to calm down. Turn your life around as I did, and do something constructive with all that energy of yours, like build a doll house out of popsicle sticks or make a cardboard hat. Then maybe, after you've done some growing, mentally and spiritually, we can talk about getting you into some real yoga classes. Sound good?

Your friend[137] and[138] protector[139] of[140] the[141] Earth's[142] life[143] force,[144]

Diane[145] Patton[146]

---

[137] I want to kill that bitch, Diane.

[138] No, you don't.

[139] What!

[140] You're going to finish your book.

[141] Francine! I love you so much!

[142] I love you too, Robert.

[143] So how are we going to get her back?

[144] That's the thing—we're not, because Diane's just trying to work out her own stuff, and that doesn't have anything to do with you. Besides, she's retarded. Robert, you will succeed where your parents and neighbors didn't. You will use your power to become the sweetest ninja ever. Do you understand?

[145] Are you my real mom?

[146] No, way! We're homies!

Ninja Mind Control

With only their minds, ninjas can cloud people's heads with a thunderstorm of fists or a sprinkle of kisses. So when ninjas want something and don't feel like killing someone to get it, they use mind control. Ninjas don't have to ask for permission for anything. If they want to take yoga classes, they just go. Picture some ninja just walking in to class and everybody looks up and doesn't move, except for the guy shaking because of fear. Oh, you don't want to let me join yoga? Oh, really. You think I'm too wild? Is that it? I'm sorry to hear that. Well, how about I poke your teeth with a pencil or munch on your face as I sing about your stupidity—like how you thought sponges came from the ocean? You're so stupid and everybody knows it, even though they won't say it to your face.

Ninjas can do this kind of thing because they can control people's minds with magic. Don't believe me? Then check out how this ninja gets his way:

Ninja: Yo.
Pedestrian: Hi.
Ninja: Maybe it would be nice to give me that basketball?
Pedestrian: I don't think so. Get your own.
Ninja: But I like yours.

Pedestrian: Maybe you should . . . wait, is that a candy bar?
Ninja: Maybe.
Pedestrian: What are you going to do with it?

I think we all know what happened to the basketball. But look, my main point is that if you see a ninja, you might end up losing a bunch of your bodily possessions. So don't say I didn't warn you. There's always a price for hanging out with someone *too cool*.[147] Good[148] luck,[149] friend.[150] Good[151] luck.[152]

---

[147] Robert, I was thinking we could try something different. I want you to look at the girl in this photograph. Can you guess what emotion she's expressing?

[148] She's hanging out, Francine. Duh!

[149] Well, hanging out isn't exactly an emotion. Does she look angry to you?

[150] She's pumped.

[151] Robert, what makes **you** so angry?

[152] I don't know.

were starting to look up for Ted and me. We even started screwing again. But, much to our discontent, a ninja kicked us in the nuts, banged our heads together, and we both feel asleep. When Ted and I woke up, we found ourselves missing our hearts, both kidneys, stomachs, colons, teeth, and wallets. I can still picture the ninja, having stapled all the organs and wallets to his completely awesome[153] uniform,[154] spinning[155] around,[156] laughing.[157]

---

[153] Do you like girls, Robert?

[154] Francine, I can't stand them! They're so weird. Plus, they're so into horses. Drawing pictures of them and always talking about them. It's pretty annoying.

[155] Do you think it would be a good to learn more about them? Would you ever like to have a girlfriend?

[156] I guess so. I mean, I'll probably have to get one before I pass on. It's part of living, I guess.

[157] Just think about it. That's all.

My Dinner with a Ninja: A Hot Babe Talks About a Hot Night

Did You Know?
Making love to a mermaid would be so awesome.

Not only do ninjas touch the lives of their victims, they also touch hot babes—A LOT. Here, some babe wrote in her diary about her dinner date with the ninja. Don't read this if you're scared of getting all hot and sweaty.

Friday, June 21, 2002

Dear Diary,

Hello. I am a hot babe. I had dinner with a ninja on Wednesday. The day started with a haircut, which a barber gave me. Then I put on perfume. After that, I tried on different dresses. The one with flowers is my favorite because my mother gave it to me. (She's dead.) Before I went over to the ninja's house, I watched TV and ate some snacks, which put me at peace. When I arrived at the ninja's hacienda, I noticed many expensive cars in the driveway. And the house was painted jet black and had gun turrets. Then, out of nowhere, the ninja opened the door and looked great. He was tall.

"Good evening, Madame," he said.

I was like, "Wow."

"Yo, do you want to come into my hacienda?"

"Hell, yeah!" I said. Then I got pumped. The house smelled awesome and there was some badass music playing. Money was just lying on the couch and nobody cared. Even the carpet was leather. To my surprise, the ninja prepared a dream dinner—it was spicy chili. And instead of plates, we used diapers, which is romantic, if you ask me. During dinner the ninja had amazing things to say about back flips and video games—I was flabbergasted. And when coins from my pocket fell between the couch, I didn't even care, because I was falling in love. Out of nowhere, we started making out, hard. Then I woke up in a ditch. It was great. I'll never forget it.

Apparently, the girl still talks about the ninja whenever anyone comes to the house to visit. And a couple weeks later, there was this guy who tried to date her, but she didn't want anything to do with a man who's afraid[158] to[159] express[160] his[161] feelings[162] and[163] get[164] pumped.[165]

---

[158] Excuse me. EXCUSE ME! I would like a sentence or paragraph with you.

[159] What.

[160] IS THIS YOUR BOOK? I found this piece of crap RIGHT WITHIN THE REACH OF MY KIDS! I don't want them to reading this kind of stuff.

[161] Wait! You actually read my book?

[162] Yeah, so?

[163] Really? The whole thing?

[164] I read everything. Even the poem about the hippos that appeared nice and normal but really weren't, which was pure evil.

[165] Cool.

Romance and Ninjas

Ninjas are amazing lovers. Before porking, a ninja will generally get underneath the covers while his mate changes her dirty underpants in the bathroom. Then, when she's all cleaned up, she gets under the covers, too. Then they'll stare at each other for a couple seconds and wonder how it finally came to this. Then the ninja will approach the female. She will look scared, but so will he. Then this soft music will happen, but nobody will care. Then they hug. And the lights go out. They just lie there talking about who threw up during lunch or if they saw a fight on the bus. And when they wake up in the morning, they eat breakfast off each other's stomachs, and that's it!

I'm practicing to be romantic, too. Francine and I found an erotic massage book underneath Mom's magazines. I've already practiced on some of the animals in the neighborhood. I rub them down pretty good. Some even moan. Anyways, to get you in the mood, I wrote down some romantic stories that turn on ninjas. The following soap operas are like fables, but hotter. The first is about a single mother trying to make it in the big city without comprising her hot body. The second is about balancing a love-life and kids in the big city. And the third is about a[166] kid[167] with[168] a[169] mustache.[170]

The Smear

The camera opens slowly to reveal black smoke pretty much everywhere. And there is thunder. A single flute is pumping up the audience. Then, without a drop of preparation, the audience hears a nibbling sound. The smoke blows away to reveal a single mother breast-feeding three young boys in a badass living room. The television-audience now hears soothing music with pianos and more flutes, which will calm them. The mother is wearing an all black apron with holsters for kids. Basically she's a loner, with babies. Nobody messed with the single mom until one stupid day a killer popped a sprocket and went nuts. So the crazy killer taps on the single mother's living room door and says, "Hey, I'm going to kill you pretty soon." And she says, "By pretty soon, you mean never." But her impropriety majorly pisses off the killer. And then, out of nowhere, he opens the door. The single mom stands up, hard. And, with boys still suckling, she begins to spin on one hoof. (In slow motion, the killer's smile flips into a frown.) The boys' tiny limbs flop on the killer's face and smooshes his teeth into liquid. The killer falls backwards into a bunch of things. And flute sounds are literally out of control when the single mom smears pap all over the killer's mouth and face. But then, the audience hears a single flute wailing in the background to represent a bunch of single mothers.

---

[166] Hey John, do you have pubes?

[167] Yeah.

[168] How many?

[169] I don't know—like two thousand.

[170] Holy crap!

The End

I[171] feel[172] like[173] a[174] plum[175] exploded[176] in[177] my[178] pants.[179]

Dirty Laundry

There's a laundry mat in a horrible part of time and space. It's completely empty except for the janitor, a lady, some guy, and some kid that nobody messed with, ever. This kid is awesome. He's doing push-ups while waiting for his laundry. But he stops and flips on his back to see who's walking through the door. An amazing single mother, wearing a crotchless skirt, enters the mat. The kid is like, "Hey, you. Need some help?" And the single mother is like, "Maybe." Then they start frenching hard. Everybody tries to stop them because it's so beautiful. But, out of nowhere, the mother's children attack and screw up everything. The children are completely covered with serum, so they keep slipping out of everybody's hands. But the two people are in love and it doesn't matter. They run out of the laundry mat, *away from everyone*. Then the lovers jump on bare naked horses and ride through the forest to the top of a castle that's completely smothered with ponies and bubbles. The kid is like, "Are you ready?" And she's like, "Second base or third base?" And the kid is like,

---

[171] Ms. Evans.

[172] What!

[173] Did you like my script?

[174] It's horrible.

[175] Do you want to drink pop and hold hands all night?

[176] What! I'm a single mother of three boys! I don't need this right now!

[177] Wait! I could be their dad or something. Then we could be together forever, like friends with benefits. Is that cool?

[178] You're ten years old! I'm not *for* you! Besides, you don't need a wife or a girl-friend, you need a child psychologist.

[179] Haven't you ever been pumped about something?

"Third." So they start moaning hard, and the townspeople start yelling at the castle for them to stop, because they can't concentrate on their peasant work. So the couple keeps moaning in spite of the people, but then the peasants start yelling even louder! So the kid stops and goes out to the balcony and says he's almost done so they can wait. And all the townspeople decide to take a lunch break because it's that time anyway.

The End

Don't [180] *worry,* [181] *homey,* [182] *girls* [183] *love* [184] *this* [185] *stuff.* [186]

Mercedes

A really old mom covered with rabies trips on the sidewalk and knocks all her teeth out. Nobody will talk to her because of the smell. Plus, she was voted for having the ugliest boobs ever. While laying in a dumpster, a badass kid walks by. He has a full-blown mustache. The elderly mother stands up in the dumpster and says, "Excuse me, sir. What is your name?" And the kid says, "Go back to sleep." But the lady is like, "I'm completely awake, and fuck you." The kid says, "Whatever," which arouses her. She wants him so bad. "Please sir, I have children . . ." and three poop stained heads pop out from the garbage bin. But the kid starts to run, because he doesn't need that crap in his life, and the stupid loser/mom screams, "You can at least tell me your name!" And the kid replies, "They call me Mercedes."

---

[180] Damnit! Is that supposed to be us?

[181] Maybe.

[182] Well it's never gonna happen!

[183] But you are fully developed and—

[184] —and you are a moron.

[185] No, I'm not. I'm different than other boys my age. I can do the splits!

[186] Get the fuck out of here.

The End

Francine made up the ugliest boobs ever[187] *part.*[188] *She's*[189] *a*[190] *genius.*[191]

---

[187] Hey man, don't sweat it. There's a girl out there just for you. You just have to be patient.—**John, ed.**

[188] You mean I have to wait a couple hours.

[189] More or less.

[190] Well, there's this one girl in my class, Dawn—you don't know her. She's alright, except her right arm is all gnarled up. According to some specific parties, she told several people she likes me because of my mind, but I think it's just her vagina talking.

[191] Maybe she really likes you.

How to Tell If a Ninja Is Trying[192] to[193] Kill You or Trying to Hang Out with You

---

Did You Know?
Dear badass dogs of planet Earth,
I like you.

If you suspect that a ninja is around your neighborhood, then you might want to find out if they want to murder you OR just hang out. Once, there was this kid who thought that a ninja wanted to chill with him—so he hung himself from a tree hoping the ninja

---

[192] Dude, this isn't entirely correct. With what you said so far, stating that ninjas *try* may lead to some inconsistency. Trying implies a possibility of failure and that would contradict the sweetness of the ninja. Consider whether a ninja may fail to hang out with another person: if that person has a free will, they could choose not to hang out with the ninja. In such a case there is the possibility that the ninja fails to hang out with someone with which they choose to hang. Since the ninja fails, he's not that sweet. But many who give this particular argument fail to account for the Total Sweetness of the ninja. A few people have tried to resist hanging out with a ninja, but have always failed. The pure sweetness germinating from the ninja makes it impossible to resist their temptation. People may have other motives contrary to hanging out with the ninja, but these motives are infinitely weaker than the motive to be near such Total Sweetness. Furthermore, with Total Sweetness in mind, consider this corollary: if we take the garden variety conception of free will, where there must be at least two possible choices for one to freely choose, then free will is non-existent. There is only one possible choice, if a ninja wants to hang out with you, you must hang out. Therefore, because of the total sweetness of the ninja, the general conception of free will is lacking and a more sophisticated version is required for a coherent theory of free will.—**John, ed.**

[193] If a ninja wanted to hang with me, I'd be like, "Yes." Man, I wish there were some ninjas around here to chill with. I wish I could go find some.

would come save him to hang out. But yeah right, all the ninja did was tickle his feet while he starved for breath. Somebody messed up. But what's worse is that this one girl thought a ninja wanted to murder her, so she mailed herself to a space colony, started a new life there, and met a seemingly nice man who would later make her feel unappreciated and fat. But the ninja down on Earth only wanted to gossip and talk about horses and that's it! So if you too suspect that a ninja is around town, then you need to think first before you do anything. Fortunately, Francine and I created this short list of things to help you out, but it's not complete, because ninjas are pretty creative. Knowledge, my friend, is the key to living *or* dying.

A ninja is trying to hang out with you if . . .	A ninja is trying to kill you if . . .
There are poop sprinkles in your underpants.	Those poop sprinkles in your underpants are glass.
After pausing your video game and eating lunch, you come back and see that the game has advanced past the part you could never, ever beat.	After returning to your game, you see that you lost all your lives and somebody bukkakied on the TV.
You find a can of beer in your pillow case.	You find a can of root beer in your pillow case.
When you eat chocolate ice cream, it tastes like spicy chili.	When you eat chocolate ice cream, it tastes like a colon.
While sleeping in a sleeping bag, you eventually wake up.	You just keep sleeping.
When playing at a friend's house, you end up staying up till you can't play anymore or just just fall asleep.	When playing at your buddy's place, your mom calls for you to come home, but she sounds super scared.
Inside your lunch bag, you find amazing candy treats that would make even the strongest kid drip urine.	In your lunch bag, you find raw carrots and dandruff.
While picking your nose, you find a chocolate chip.	While picking your nose, you find a chocolate chip.

Dealing with Ninjas on a Personal Level

If a ninja wants to kill you there's pretty much nothing you can do. You can tell all your family that you hate them before you go, but that's about it. But if you think you're lucky, you could try putting a bowl of chili outside your window. If a ninja is about to kill you and he's sneaking through your window, he might see the chili, eat it, and come inside your room and hug you while you're sleeping, holding you in his arms, rocking you back and forth, wishing for a better life for you, somewhere far away from here. If this happens, then just lie there and enjoy it. And don't move either, because I heard that there was one kid who woke up and the ninja was really embarrassed, and it got pretty weird for everybody involved.

Other than that, there isn't much you can do. And don't try to run either, 'cause it won't work—these guys are ninjas. But let's say a ninja *does* want to hang out with you. What if you screw up and look like a moron? Then what? Nobody's going to like you, that's what. Here's a little guide to dealing with ninjas when you encounter one:

Arranging Rides

If a ninja can't get over to your house, he can't hang out with you. It sounds simple, but people often forget. Ask your mom if she'll pick him up. If she can't, then ask if the ninja can get a ride over if your mom will give him a ride home. As long as one parent isn't doing all the driving, no one's going to feel overburdened.

Conversation

Now, after saying hello, you need to keep the conversation going. Don't just sit there and stare at him, no matter how awesome he is. Ninjas know how sweet they are, and they don't need people telling them every second. Try to bring up topics they enjoy, even if you're not into it that much, like spacecrafts, dead people, or fire. Act interested in what they're talking about— this will make them want to be with you and hang out next time you ask. Here are some questions you can use to get the conversation started:

- What's your favorite weapon?
- Do you use evil or good magic? Why?

- What's the dumbest thing you ever heard somebody say?
- Oh, man that would be so awesome to kill people for money. Dude, how many people have you killed? Were you scared?
- What type of music are you into?
- Are you having any trouble at home?

Sharing

Now a ninja might want to play with your things. Let him, because even if he breaks your stuff it can be replaced, but your life cannot. BUT if he gets too pushy and doesn't give you a turn, you need to say something like, "Umm. Hello. I would like to play with that *now*." 'Cause, if you act like a wimp, the ninja will think you're worthless, because you don't have anyone else and you really need this. By acting like a wimpy baby, you give the ninja permission to mistreat you. And that doesn't have to happen.

Acting Cool

Once you get a ninja in your room, don't lose it and start screaming out the window for your friends to come over and look at him. That would be pretty annoying, especially if a ninja just wants to chill. Just pretend that it's cool that he came over and you're not going to crap your pants about it. Put on some music and make sure that you relax, too. Remember, it's your house! A lot of people forget that when they have guests over, and they end up not enjoying themselves at all. But the whole point of hanging out is having fun.

Also, pretend that this type of thing happens a lot. And think of some cool stuff to say like, "Yo, there's this guy in my school, he says he can hold his breath for over twenty minutes, but nobody believes him." And tell the ninja about cool stuff you can do, without sounding like you're bragging, like, "Yo, one time I kicked a soccer ball so hard it knocked out this kid's retainer. Everybody was laughing their asses off. It was pretty awesome.

You should have been there." Now, that one got me invited to a barmitzvah once, but you can't use it—that's my line.[194]

Petting

After you guys have hung out for a couple hours, a ninja might try to sniff your hand. Don't freak out. He's just getting to know you. You must speak softly in a lovely voice. This will put him at ease. And don't make any sudden moves. Now, when petting, make sure to hold your hand PALM DOWN. If you have your palm up, he might think you're going to hit him, because someone might have hit him in the past. Then you can begin to pet. Make sure to go with the fur, otherwise they might get colicky. After you're done petting, wash your hands. You can pick up diseases from their fur, like *E. coli*.[195] So don't forget to wash your fingers, before stuffing them back in your mouth.

Attire

Ninjas are attracted to shiny things, like freshly washed cans or medallions. So don't wear anything like that, since they might chew on it. I don't understand why this happens.

---

[194] There was this one kid in my class that was really into robots. I don't know what his deal was, but it was pretty annoying. That's all he would talk about. We could be talking about girls, and he'd start talking about how awesome it would be to have a robot girlfriend that you could make love to, and she wouldn't ever make fun of you 'cause that's how she was programmed. Even though a robot girl sounded cool, nobody could stand being around him for longer than a minute. And I hated him too, because he said I was his only friend. He'd always ask to hang out, but I would say I had to do chores or something, which was true, but I would have lied if it weren't. One day, we were all playing soccer. He picked me to be on his team. And, not surprisingly, during the whole game he pretended to be a robot: he'd walk real slow and make beeping sounds, like we weren't trying to win or anything! I pulled him off the field and told him, "Act like a kid and stop obsessing over something so frigg'n stupid. Who gives a crap about robots, anyway? You're no robot. You're a fucking nobody!" I wanted to help him, but he started to cry, which made me madder and, before I knew it, I was hitting him in the face. I just wanted him to play soccer and act like a normal kid.

[195] *E. coli* stands for *Escherichia coli*. It's basically a virus that can get into your stomach and make trouble. Encyclopedia Britannica, Volume E.

Feeding

Ninjas' favorite foods are sushi, egg rolls, chicken, curry, tacos, pizza, leaves, apples, and spicy-chili. Most of the time, a ninja only wants the food in your hand, but if your fingers get in the way, they might eat them, too! They might not know where the taco ends and your fingers begin. So DON'T CURL YOUR FINGERS while feeding. Keep your hand spread wide open.

Don't!   **Do—oh man, look how flat that hand is.**

Saying Goodbye

Everything may be going pretty sweet when hanging out with a ninja, but if you screw it up at the end by saying something completely stupid, it's over. Ninjas remember the last few moments the best—so they've got to count, hard. After you both get tired playing or watching TV, walk the ninja to the door and *talk about something sweet that happened during the visit* so he can think about it on the ride home and really understand how cool it is to be with you. And don't get all sad and beg him to stay longer. He might start thinking that you're desperate. Only after he's left the driveway, can you close the door and fall back against it, and rock back and forth, thinking about all the stuff you guys did, wishing, hoping, praying that it will all happen again. And if you did all the crap I just told you, it probably will.

PART IV

Welcome to My Dojo!

A medieval warrior said to his son, "It is not good to be crazy. Before you get crazy, count to one hundred, or I'll uppercut you." Then one day, the kid got a little crazy and warrior dad looked right at him and the kid started counting, but instead of relaxing, he got even more pumped, and by the time he hit twelve, the kid went bananas and started spanking his dad and he couldn't stop. And when his dad was lying on the ground screaming, "WHY?" the kid whispered, "Because I can."

—Ancient Chinese Proverb

Ƴou might be asking yourself, "Good evening, how is this ancient Chinese or Japanese tradition or whatever going to help me, a modern person with guns and television?" Well, you know what? This stuff has lasted 2,500 years because IT'S AWESOME, THAT'S WHY! And frankly, whether or not you think ninjas are sweet doesn't matter. What matters is that they could beat your ass. And if that doesn't make sense to you, nothing will.

Nevertheless, after seeing a bunch of ninja and kung fu movies, a lot of people think that they'll get magical powers if they become a ninja. Well, you know what, they're right. There have been news reports of kids flying around cities, kicking soccer balls into space, and ripping off their dad's spanking arm. All because they decided to become ninjas. BUT making the decision to be a ninja can be a super hard one. Your friends and relatives may tell you that you should be a mailman or a doctor. They might say that you're not good enough, or even that you're too fat or uptight. But if you want to be a ninja, I mean really, really want to be one, then you have to do it. You just have to, no matter what. But you also have to know for sure. So you should learn about other types of jobs to see what you're missing.

Lawyers

Lawyers just hang out in courtrooms all day and, during recess, they don't even get to go outside! They have to take a bunch of crap from the judge who doesn't even care about them. And nobody should have to go through that.

Doctors

Doctors are retarded. They don't do anything. Sometimes they cut people, which is cool, but they don't do it enough. And when they actually do kill somebody, everybody yells at them. Plus, you have to look at guys' wieners all day—so forget it.

Fishermen

All they do is sit in a boat and look at each other all day, and their socks are always wet. Nobody likes them, because they can't figure out what they want out of life and probably never will.

Mailmen   Retarded

Veterinarian   O.K., because the dogs flow like wine, which is awesome, but other than that, it's retarded

Painter   Boring

Astronaut   Float around in a spaceship with a bunch of naked guys? NO WAY!

Clerk   Retarded

Sailor   Double retarded

Now, after I told you all that crap, I want you to sit back and really think about it. It may take days or even weeks, but at least you'll know for sure.

O.K., done? 'Cause I know I am. Now do you still wanna be a ninja? Do you think you have what it takes? I am going to show you the lefts and rights of the art of killing people and looking sweet. A ninja needs spirit, skills, weapons, a suit, and moves. And guess what? I am going to teach you all that crap right now. But . . . before we get to the real training, we have to do something. (I think you know what that is.)

Pump-Up Part II:

More Movie Scripts That Make Me and Francine Bite Each Other Hard

Nobody can be a ninja if they're not pumped—nobody. And if you're still not pumped up, then you're a moron. Luckily, I can help. I wrote three more scripts to really get you pumped. On the top, these movies may appear foolish or dumb, but as you'll see, the characters in them are pretty cool, and work on many levels, because they pump you up. *The King's Gold/Babes* is about teamwork and friendship. *The Pirate Dance* is about danger, brotherhood, and the pure stupidity of pirates. And the third script, *Little Tiny Hippo*, is about a little tiny hippo.

The King's Gold/Babes

SCENE 1:
In the olden days, there was this sweet king that had mounds of gold and babes. But then these pirates decide to steal the mounds and surround the castle and everybody freaks, except the king, who is like, "Chill homies, I'll handle this crap."

The pirates stand outside the castle walls and are like, "You think you are so cool, but guess what, you're not. Good luck dying!" Then the king replies, "Yeah, right. How would you like to meet my best friends?"

Then, out of nowhere, there is a small sound of a guitar wailing really, really hard behind the hills. The wailing starts getting louder and louder and louder. Then, out of nowhere, there is this one sweet-ass ninja standing on top of a huge hill. Everybody is like, "Wooooooooooooow!" He is wearing all black and he has this jet-red guitar in his hands. Then smoke smokes over the hills like trains. But the smoke is ninjas. And the pirates see about a billion ninjas with guitars standing on top this his huge hill. And they start to wail . . .

When the ninjas wail on their guitars, the pirates spray diarrhea on each other and love it. And when they wail harder, the pirates spray harder. As the ninjas saunter down the hill, the pirates' chests and butts explode. (Basically, they're dead or about to die.) Then the ninjas finally reach the boss pirate who is *really* huge. Out of nowhere, the boss pirate pulls out this baby banjo and tries to fiddle with it like a little, retarded baby. The ninjas are like, "Yeah, right," and all the billions of ninjas surround the boss pirate. Half of the ninjas all combine to form the biggest guitar in the universe. The other half form the second biggest boner in the universe. Then the huge guitar points right at the pirate, who is like "Holy CRAAAAAAAAAAAAAAAAAAAAAP!" Before the pirate could even do anything, the super boner slaps against the guitar, making the hugest wail ever to happen anywhere ever. The pirate explodes so hard that every single one of his kids he would have had explodes and all of his grandparents explode along with his neighbors and even people who he merely said "Hello" to.

Then there is a huge concert at the castle. All the babes in the castle morph into this humongous female crotch. The huge boner and crotch pork softly, while slamming into the guitar and wailing. And guess what, the king sits on top of this huge pile of gold and babes and laughs his frigg'n ass off about how stupid the pirates were.

The End

I don't know about you, but after reading this script, I splashed all the water out of the tub.

The Pirate Dance
(Blood Brothers in the Japanese version)

SCENE 1:

The scene opens up with some soft annoying music to get the audience super pissed. The camera shows a bunch of pirates eating chicken buttholes. But, fortunately, a ninja sees everything and realizes what a bunch of *bullcrap* it is. So this one ninja walks up to them and is like, "Yo, what's your problem?" The camera zooms directly on a pirate's mouth, which states, "Get out of here now," and chicken buttholes fall all over the silverware. Then the camera cuts to the ninja's mouth which says, "No," but it looks cool. The audience then sees the ninja pull out a huge guitar and he starts to wail. But the pirates don't explode, they start to dance . . . hard. And when they dance, the pirates look like a bunch of crabby moms. Everybody in the entire world craps their pants laughing at the pure stupidity of the pirates. But the ninja has A.D.D. and starts losing energy/power and the pirates start stopping dancing. (There will be some suspense filled violins and guitars playing so that the audience gets scared and/or scared-pumped.) In several motions, the pirates come toward the ninja. BUT, out of nowhere, this badass lake appears and a huge hippo busts out of it hard. Water sprays everywhere, including the pirates' shirts (which causes their boobs to just barely appear through the soft cloth). The pirates are like, "This can't be happening!" And the hippo says, "Guess what? . . . IT is," and slaps five with the ninja pretty hard. Then the ninja says, "Let's rock, brother." And they both pull out expensive guitars and start wailing on them really, really hard. Since the ninja can't concentrate, the hippo thoughtfully guides his hand, because they are blood brothers till the end of space and time. Then the pirates all morph into this giant diaper and the hippo and ninja morph into a super poop-filled baby that takes the biggest frigg'n dump in the pirate/diaper. The pirates' scream turns into a crap-gargle (this will make audience laugh gregariously). The ninja's A.D.D. heals and the two buddies/brothers smoke cigarettes and get ice cream and pop, which they enjoy a lot.

The End

I don't know how anybody can tolerate pirates after reading this stuff.

Little Tiny Hippo

SCENE 1:
There is this chubby, little tiny hippo who is hyperactive and has A.D.D., gappy teeth, and everybody thinks he's crazy but he really isn't. His name is Roberq and he doesn't have any friends because he gets too pumped sometimes. One day Roberq is just hanging around a lake (like usual) making up stories and goofing around, not hurting any other hippos and stuff. Then some pirate starts beating his ass bad, which royally sucks. Roberq tries to run away, but can't because the pirate calls a bunch of his buddies to help out. One pirate is in the shape of a dad; another pirate is in the shape of some friend who never wants to hang out 'cause you accidentally screwed up once; and the last pirate is in the shape of a stupid mom with three kids. Roberq's only this little tiny hippo and everybody is completely beating his ass and he didn't do any-

thing. It's like these pirates don't even understand what it's like to be a hippo. But guess what, Roberq hears this trumpet in the background that sounds exactly like a guitar. (And the camera spams up to see about a trillion ninjas flying in the air like geese in guitar formation.) The pirates are like, "Nobody can stop us, because we're <u>adults</u>!" And out of nowhere, the pirates hear this little tiny voice that says, "Yeah, right." It is the little tiny hippo! The pirates are surprised by the hippo's audacity, yet totally willing to continue beating his ass worse than before. And just when the pirates are about to begin again, they start to feel little poop droppings on their necks and shoulders. (They are ninja droppings with acid and poison.) The pirates start sizzling like tube steak. Then all the ninjas land and completely surround the pirates. One ninja steps forward and is like, "Maybe you should get a life, and by life I mean death." (The pirates are completely speechless.) Then that ninja starts beating the pirates' asses bad— so bad that people in other dimensions start feeling sorry for them. When the ninja finishes, which was about a billion years later, the next ninja starts. All one-trillion ninjas beat the pirates' asses. So for one billion trillion years this goes on. And if you're ever alone in the forest and you listen closely, you can still hear the little tiny hippo saying, "Yeah, right."

To be continued . . .

Do You Have the Ninja Spirit?

Did You Know?

Here is a list of particularly awesome things:
  dogs
  sniping
  very spicy chili
  cat claws on people (but still cool on cats)

Becoming a ninja is like making a fort. You set up some chairs and get a huge blanket to throw over the chairs. You put couch cushions on the sides to make walls and a door. But be sure to make a small opening near the entrance to see who wants to come in. And don't use a blanket that's too heavy or else it will sink in the middle. Make sure that dogs know where to get in, too. And that's about it!

By following the magic tripod of Goal Setting, Determination, and Attitude, you will develop REAL ninja spirit to base all your ninja skills on. And you'll need to build a badass foundation if you want to succeed, trust me.[196]

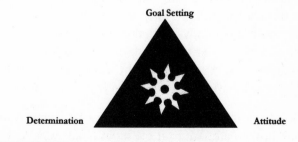

Goal Setting

Determination   Attitude

---

[196] Don't believe me? Check out this note where Maria McGillis talks about me. I'm famous! See **Exhibit C**, in *Appendix and Exhibits*.

Goal setting

I get a lot of questions about whether girls or women can be ninjas. Well, anybody can be a ninja if they feel it in their heart. You just have to look within yourself and try to figure out what's really important to YOU. Think about this: Are you living the life your parents wanted to live? What goals do you have? Are these goals yours or are they someone else's? Are you so dependant on another person that you don't know who you are or what you want? Most importantly, ask yourself what would you do with your life if you could do anything you wanted regardless of what other people might think? Your answer is what you *should* be doing, since this is what you really want to do. If deep within your catacombs, you feel that your destiny is to be a ninja, then that's what you have to do. And it doesn't matter what anybody else thinks.

Determination

Becoming a ninja isn't easy. You'll get tired. You'll get colicky. But in the end, you'll be pretty sweet. And even though it's hard work, you can't go around complaining. There's this one kid I know who can't stop whining because his dad ran away from home and never sends him cards or sings happy birthday. I don't know what his problem is—my ultimate dream is to have a dead-beat dad. It just sounds dangerous. Nevertheless, besides porking (really) hot babes, flipping out, wailing on guitars, and cutting off heads, a ninja has to train. They have to meditate ALL THE TIME. But most importantly, each morning a ninja should think about going a little crazier than the day before. Beyond thinking about going berserk, a ninja must, by definition, actually go berserk. Here are a few starters if you don't know where to begin:

1. Look for a mom and baby enjoying a hot summer afternoon in the park. Wait till the mom looks away and then start frenching that baby, hard. Then when the mom turns around, frigg'n book.

2. Go hide near the patio of a restaurant. Look for the hungriest dude you can find. Wait till he gets his food and then, when he's just about to take a bite, grab the plate and frigg'n book!

3. Get a huge squirt gun and go to the zoo. Find the biggest, craziest gorilla there and squirt him in the face, hard. Stand around and continue squirting until the gorilla *completely* freaks out. Then throw a ladder in the cage so he can climb out. But this time don't stand around. Frigg'n book!

4. Go to the theater by yourself. Sit behind a family. Locate their popcorn tub. Take off one of your socks, roll up your pant leg, and wait till the climax of the movie. Now swing your leg over the seat with your toes pointed downward and plunge your foot into the popcorn. Depending on how pumped you are, do one of the following: If you're super pumped, leave your foot in the tub as long as you can; if you're just kinda pumped, apologize and say it was a simple accident.

Attitude (or, as the French call it, Pizzas)

A ninja has got to have attitude—that is, a ninja must be ready at any moment to chill the fuck out whatever the situation may be. Nobody, I mean nobody, can chill like a ninja. Just lay back, call some homies, and chill. Or call some honies, if need be.

Now go out there and be a ninja. This stuff is what dreams are made of. Stick to your goals and go live your dream.[197] Thank[198] you.[199]

---

[197] Now, Robert. I was thinking we could try out a little exercise. This may sound strange, but I want you to draw an Easter egg—however you like. Just let yourself go free, wherever it takes you. Find that scary place and explore so you don't feel afraid anymore.

[198] Oh. O.K., Francine. Where do you want me to draw the egg?

[199] Right here, in your book!

200

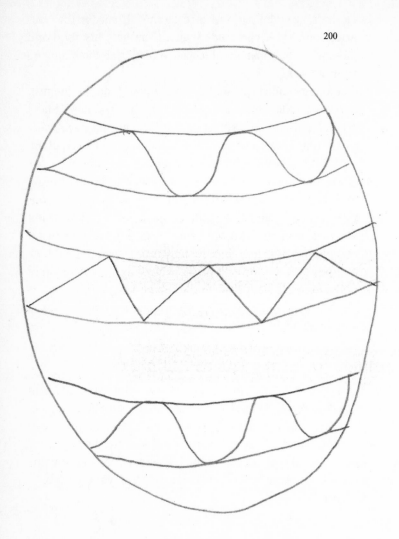

---
200 O.K., that's a start. But I want you to really explore. Really explore!

201

I feel good

---

[201] Better, a little crazy, but that's O.K. Try harder. Squeeze it out of yourself.

202

202 Wait. What's going on! Who's that? Is that you? Squeeeeeeeeeeeeeeze!

203

---

[203] Holy crap! Who are you, Robert Hamburger?

I'M
PROBABLY
A NINJA!

Becoming a Ninja

Did You Know?

In the past, ninjas would dip their hands and feet into pure lava to make them hard. They don't do that anymore, because where do you get lava?

To[204] become[205] a[206] ninja[207], you[208] have[209] to[210] perfect[211] your[212] skills.[213] Otherwise, you're just another guy in black pajamas. Below, I will teach you how to master sleeping, stealth, patience, hiding, getting respect, and building energy. Let's get started.

Get Enough Sleep

Even though ninjas don't have a set bedtime, they still believe in sleeping. Because if they're too tired during a mission, they might end up making a silly mistake. Personally, I have to go to bed at 6:00 P.M. every night. I'm not a big fan of going to bed early, but

---

[204] Dammit, Robert, you are NOT a ninja! Get the wig.

[205] No!

[206] What?

[207] I said, no!

[208] Get over here, you fucking retard.

[209] Now, put on the wig!

[210] No! It itches. Ahhhhh, my nipples!

[211] Now, get in the box!

[212] Can I keep the lid open this time?

[213] Shut up!

it's Dad's number one rule. I hated it at first, but during school Ms. Burbell has me run extra errands, because I have so much energy. I get them done *fast*. I like Mrs. Burbell. She's pretty funny, too. One time, she came into class one day with makeup smeared all over her face. She said that she was in the bathroom puking, because her sister died. And when Ms. Burbell said "puking," we laughed our frigg'n asses off.

Stealth

Ninjas are sneaky and pretty fast; so they can frigg'n book. Make sure you're good at this.

Hiding

During the winter, ninjas wear a white shirt and white pants so they can blend in. And during the summer, they wear a light tank top and shorts. But when hiding during the night, they wear what they had on earlier that day, because it's dark—so who cares? Hiding is just as important as stealth. They go together like ninjas and guitars. If you have to spy on a victim for hours, you should be hiding—otherwise it's more like staring, which gets weird after a while. A ninja can hide in anything: closets, toy boxes, backpacks, lockers, whatever. If you want to be a ninja you have got to practice hiding everywhere. And make sure to bring some blankets and a pillow. You might be hiding for over ten minutes and the ground might make your butt sore. Don't forget some treats either, because you might get hungry and your victim may hear your stomach moan and he'll look around to investigate.

Patience

If a ninja wants to kill somebody, they might have to wait for them to look the other way, which may take a super long time. So a ninja must have patience or they will screw everything up. One time I hid under Mom's bed all day and peed in a sandwich bag just so I could freak out my aunts when they were changing their panties. But Dad got real mad, because he was embarrassed. And he made me wear the bag to school, which I'm going to tell a therapist when I'm older. He's thinks he's so frigg'n important because his job is to make sure that the tuna that goes on the boat equals the tuna coming off, but nobody even cares. One time, he came home smelling like fish super bad and I accidentally covered my nose and then when he saw, he kicked me in the nuts. The best example of patience is old people. They have **a lot** of patience. That's probably why they can sit on the toilet for over an hour. I don't how they can do that. There are some things you can do to increase your patience, but I forgot them. I guess you just relax.

Energy/Power

A good ninja always needs energy to flip out. So always keep some treats in your bag for energy.

But most importantly, you need to keep alert, 'cause you never know what's going to happen next, and you've got to keep cool. Like this one time in class, I was just talking to the guy next to me and, guess what, there were these rich kids sitting in front of class who were shooting spitballs all over the place. One of them shot a spitball at me and it went straight into my mouth! But I just swallowed it and kept talking like nothing happened. It was already in there—so I didn't want to make a big deal about it. The kids freaked out and didn't mess with me again. So always be ready, because that sort of thing could happen to anyone.

To practice all your ninja skills together, here's an official test:

1. Find some people.
2. Make sure they're preoccupied—maybe they're looking at the ocean or writing a poem.
3. Sneak up behind them and squat down.

4. Now, try to fit one of their fingers all the way into your mouth without them knowing it.

5. Run.

If you succeed, you are mastering the ninja skills, which[214] is[215] a[216] good[217] thing.[218]

---

[214] John, you've got to get me out of here. I've got to escape. They only keep me around so they can claim me as a dependant on their taxes. Don't believe me? Look at **Exhibit E**! Can you drive me to the bus station or something? I'm going to Japan/China.

[215] I don't know, man. That would be kidnapping and I can't get anything else on my record.

[216] It's not kidnapping when the kid wants to go!

[218] Can't you wait a couple years till they grow out of it? Just try to stay out of their way and keep quiet till you're old enough to move out on your own. It worked for me.

[218] I have to go, John. I'm a ninja and stuff. Are you going to help me?

Porking

Ninjas don't hold hot babes and listen to them complain all night—they pork them. BUT, before a ninja can pork a hot babe, they have get them all hot and ready. They do this through romance, telling them compliments about their blouse, or buying them a dinner platter. But if you don't want to do any of that stuff, then here are some tips to be romantic like a ninja:

- Pull her hair, but not too hard.
- Wear cologne. Put some on neck and wrists. You can also put some on your shirt.
- Pretend you don't like her, 'cause if she knows you like her, then you can forget it.
- Make sure you have clean underwear and if you don't, just turn a dirty pair inside out.
- Talk to other girls right in front of her face.
- Get her to notice you—wear brightly colored clothing or a tall hat.
- Find someone weaker than you and make him look dumb.
- Follow her home and watch out for her, like if some robber tries to attack her, you would just be there, jumping down from a tree, scratching his face, all the while telling her, "Relax and keep calm, I've got everything under control." But if you end up killing the guy and she passes out, just pick her up in your arms and carry her to her house and leave the girl on the porch. Make sure to wrap her up in a blanket and leave a plate of warm food in case she gets hungry. Then, before you leave, put a note underneath her hand that says, "Don't worry about anything. He will never hurt you again. I cut him up pretty good. If you need

anything else, just give me a call. Robert." But use your name instead, and USE CURSIVE—that stuff is romantic. Then she's yours.

Now, if you do all that stuff I told you and you finally get the girl into the basement, you can dry ride her—it's like making out, but without the commitment. Here's how:

1. Find someone you like more than a friend, but less than a wife.
2. Hang out with them around two-and-a-half times.
3. Wait till there are no adults around.
4. Rub your crotches together while wearing pants.
5. Leave the premises.

And if somebody's dad comes home, you can stop immediately without a problem—so, who cares!

A Ninja Makes a Telephone Call

Guy: Hello.

Ninja:

Guy: Who is this?

Ninja: Nobody.

Guy: No, really. Who is this?

Ninja: Don't worry about it.

Guy: Do you want to die or something?

Ninja: Maybe.

Guy: Then why don't you come over and fight me, since you seem to be such an expert on being so tough?

Ninja: Make me.

Guy: You called me. So let's do it.

Ninja: If we fight, you die.

Guy: Wait. Could you hold on a second? I have another call.

Ninja: Of course.

Guy: Hey, I got to go.

Ninja: What happened?

Guy: It's somebody for my mom.

Ninja: O.K. Bye.

Joining a Ninja Clan

Did You Know?

In the olden days, ninjas would develop their
strength by wrestling with dogs, playing video
games, and just plain hanging out. Fortunately,
not much has changed.

In each ninja clan, there is a division of power. Bosses are at the
top. Usually there's only one ninja boss, because it's easier that
way, but sometimes there's more if nobody wins the fight (draw).
Then there's a secretary who writes down what they talk about in
meetings, not secrets though—that would be insane. And the rest
of the ninjas are regular ninjas. You can either work alone or you
can join a clan. Sometimes, it's good to join a clan, because
you can exchange weapons when you get bored of yours, and you
can also change home base every couple days or so. But if you
work alone, you don't have to vote on anything. Plus, you can
make your own hours. And if you don't need anyone in your life,
then it's probably best to work by yourself. Plus, it's pretty diffi-
cult to join a clan. First, you've got to know other ninjas, and
that's tough for the obvious reasons. And then you have to get
them to like you, which is almost impossible if your mom doesn't
even like you.

Not everybody can handle joining a ninja clan, though. To
get in, you have to eat burning charcoal and pick up hot pans
with your bare hands or you can just stick your head in boiling
grease for two seconds.

A lot of people recommend finding a clan that's older than
you, because they can teach you a lot about sniping and secret
paths, but those clans are really hard to get into. Besides, sometimes it's better to join a clan of people younger than you, because

you can take over since you're probably bigger than everybody else. Then they'll be your personal servants, and you can make them carry you to your next victim and everything.

There was a younger clan in the neighborhood. I talked to them a couple times, but they were pretty disorganized. So I didn't even bother. But there was another one that was better, and I asked the leader whether he knew anything about ninjas. He said, "Yeah." and I was like, "Can you back it up?" and he said, "Maybe." So I really wanted to get in. But, then, they said I would probably get too excited and screw up a mission. So I was like, "COME ON!" and he was like, "No way! Look how you're acting now." And I was like, "This *is* how ninjas act!" And he was like, "No." That's O.K., though, because there's no way I could take someone like that seriously.

It doesn't matter anyway, I choose to work on my own because I don't like explaining myself, and I always end up doing all the work anyway. So to start your own ninja clan, you have to have a base. It can either be in the woods or made out of blankets. It *has* to be accessible for dogs that want to be a part of it. You've got to have weapons, which I'll talk about later. And you've got to be a[219] ninja.[220] And[221] that's[222] it![218]

---

[219] I was thinking, Robert. If you weren't so pumped all the time, then maybe you wouldn't get yourself in all the trouble that you do.—**John, ed.**

[220] Are you serious?

[221] Listen, man. One time I was applying for jobs and I thought that if I acted like myself, then they'd think I was cool and hire me. But if they didn't like it, then I wouldn't want to work there anyway. So I showed up to the interview wearing a diaper with a matching baby-bonnet. And needless to say, I didn't get the job or any other job when I acted like that. It's just that you have to sometimes hide those things about yourself that people don't like. Don't get me wrong. You don't have to act that way *all the time*. You can express yourself when you're alone in your room, but otherwise you won't be able to fit in. And sometimes fitting in is important. So, for your own sake, maybe you should try expressing your love for ninjas quietly or in a more constructive way, and maybe you could try not to be so pumped up all the time. Maybe you would have gotten into that ninja clan if you were a little calmer.

[222] Are you sure, John? It just doesn't feel right.

[223] It's just a thought.

The Cooldown Part

There are different ways of expressing oneself. Take my dad, for example. When we go to a Mexican restaurant he will always ask for the hottest sauce. He says, "Get me the stuff that the chef keeps underneath the front seat of his car." And the waiters would get really scared and hold each other's hands when Dad would splash his food with it. And then, out of nowhere, sweat would drip all over the table cloth. Sometimes he would even cry. I guess that how he dealt with life or something. Sometimes, I wish that Dad would talk more, express his feelings. But until then, I want him to just keeping eating that damn hot sauce.

Regardless, nobody can be pumped all the time. Sometimes it's nice to relax, and I can respect that. So here are a few stories to cool you down in case you have to go to bed or watch a movie or just concentrate. You can even read these with a loved one or your dog, if you like. They're beautiful.

Dog Life

There was this huge doghouse on top of a hill. Nobody had ever been in it, but people knew it was either full of ghosts or dogs. So either way, it was basically *off limits*. One simple boy was so curious that he decided to find out what was going on up there, but his sister was like, "Wake up, Zach! Let sleeping dogs or ghosts lie." And it made sense to him. So the kids never went up there. And they ended up dying when they were really old, like normal people.

Flying and Laughing

White smoke is everywhere. Plus, there's soothing music. And way up in the air, a hippo is flying and smiling down at the people below. He's laughing. Everybody is clapping, because the hippo makes them all feel so good. "That damn hippo is something else," one girl says. "He's so frigg'n nice."

"Yeah, I know. One time, my older brother went up to him and told him he was a stupid butthole right to his face. Guess what the hippo did?" said one kid.

"What?" asked the girl.

"Nothing. Isn't that hilarious? He didn't do anything."

"Are you serious? He didn't even get mad?"

"Nope. That hippo is nothing but a worthless piece of crap. He doesn't even know what it means to be alive. In fact, he's so concerned with gaining acceptance from others that he has failed to form anything resembling a personality."

"I heard he can't slam dunk either," the girl said.

"I'm not surprised."

Fields of Rice

There is this Chinese guy, right? And he's just sitting on bench. Nobody understands why he's sitting there, but he just is. Then, when a nice, happy family with a good father and good mother stroll by with their skinny, fit children, the Chinese guy looks up at them and smiles. And then BOOM! he explodes and rice flies all over the place. The family doesn't say a word and starts running. Their weekend is ruined. After everyone chills, several animals approach the bench where the rice lay. The hippos are the most scared, but also the most intrigued. They sniff, look around, and sniff some more. "What do you think?" one says. "I don't know," says another. Finally, one hippo, the brave one, whispers, "Let's eat that rice." And most do. As the rice lay in their stomachs, it wiggles, causing a warm feeling inside. They leave the scene and go back to a field where they lie down in a pile of clean grass. It's warm outside, but there is a nice breeze. They have nothing to do for the rest of the day, so they stare over the field.

Space Flip

There's these aliens who want to blow up the Earth one day. So they capture a bunch of hippos and take them up to space. The aliens are like, "Please, act like how you did on Earth so we can study you, NOW." But the hippos can't because they are so scared. They just pile up in the corner of the spaceship and moan. So the aliens fill their ship full of plants and parents and toys and lake water, but nothing seems to work. The hippos just sit on top of each other, looking out the window back at Earth, afraid of falling. But, before the hippos start to think that space sucks, they look to their left to see another animal there with them—a dog covered with human hair! The hippos and dog talk all day about dog bones and whatever hippos eat—who cares? But while the aliens are doing something stupid, the dog gives the hippos a secret note that says, *Maybe it's time that these aliens learn what hippos are all about.* After secretly reading the secret note, the hippos secretly look right in the dog's eyes. And they see flames, but those flames are really a reflection of *what's in the hippos' eyes*. Then the pump-up music really begins. The audience will see the aliens drinking coffee in the control room, laughing about how wimpy the hippos are. And they'll hear a little knock at the door. "Sounds like a wimpy knock," says one stupid alien. The music will get louder and harder when the alien walks toward the door. Then, as he opens the door, the music stops and dark smoke pours in real slow. Then a huge scream comes out from the smoke, which makes one alien spit coffee all over his bib. The hippos explode through the fog and pump-up music busts out hard, too. The hippos go nuts, like all these juices are pumping through them and it won't stop and they start rocking the space-ship, **hard**. They trample down the aliens sitting in their high chairs and smash them into the wall till their bones explode. Then the hippos run around the whole damn spaceship, causing it to flip around in space, and everything is falling off the shelves and the hippos are falling all over each other, but they don't care, because they are crazy and *they know it*. Then one hippo jumps up and grabs a chandelier and starts spinning around and screams, "Yo, homies! WE'RE GOING HOME!" The spaceship starts flipping harder and harder and its rocket boosters are going crazy and it starts crashing down toward Earth and then WHAM! they land in this gigantic pond. The door pops off and the aliens jump out because of fear, but they drown right away because they never even heard of water. Welcome to Earth, assholes. And then there is this badass guitar wailing. Wonder where that's coming from? The hippos calmly come out, one by one, all wearing sunglasses and leather jackets. They just walk out of the spaceship, smirking, and don't give a crap. But something very special happened that day. While beating the crap out of the aliens, each hippo, individually and collectively, realized the universe is there for them to

destroy and remake as their own and that to exist, they have to take responsibility for their own vibrations and energies not by controlling them, but by becoming aware of them and, most importantly, respecting them. And later, the hippos had a huge party at the lake with pizza and everything. But it ended early because some idiot kid threw a beach ball at a girl's face and her nose crumpled.

Sometimes even when a ninja is relaxed, he's pumped, because that's the way it is. And if you want nice and relaxing crap, go read another book or go to hell, 'cause[224] I'll[225] bite[226] your face off.[227]

---

[224] How do you feel, Robert?

[225] I feel—

[226] Does it feel like you've had amnesia for years and you just now remembered that you're the king of the sweetest country on Earth and you own a gigantic bicycle that can seat over a hundred people?

[227] Francine, I love you, but you need to speak English once in a while.

Ninja Kicks: Try Them Now[228]

Did You Know?

If you get in an actual fight, don't get angry because that's disrespectful, BUT if you start losing, *then* go crazy.

Remember the old saying, "If you know yourself *and* the enemy, you'll never lose. If you only know yourself, you'll win maybe half the time. BUT, if you don't know the enemy *or yourself*, you're a frigg'n idiot." Part of the ninja's nature is kicking. They can't escape it. For extended periods of time, not-kicking can often lead to resentment, guilt, and impaired relationships. So if you want to be a ninja, you've got to figure out what you need, what's important to you, and if it's kicking then you've got learn the three main kicks: the front kick, side kick, and round-house kick. Know how to do them well.

The Front Kick

One of the first kicks you should learn is the front kick. This kick is simple but complex. And it's great for nuts. Start with one foot forward, with the other eight to twelve inches behind. Keep your feet about shoulder width apart (fig. A). Put your weight on your rear leg. Lift your front knee up high (fig. B). Lean back a little bit and extend your leg, but do not hyperextend the knee (fig. C). Strike target with the ball of the foot. Return your foot to the ground so you can frigg'n run.

---

[228] For further information about kicking, please see **Exhibit D**, *Appendix and Exhibits*.

Targets: Nuts and butts

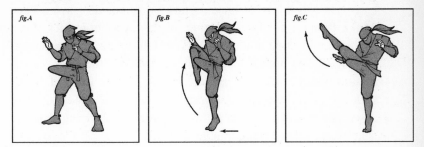

The Side Kick

Start with your feet shoulder width apart or closer (fig. A). Transfer weight to the right leg. Lift your left knee up high and inward towards your body (fig. B). Now, lean slightly to the right at the waist and rotate your right foot pointing toe away from kick. Now, extend your left leg outward, but do not hyperextend the knee (fig. C). Lower right arm to the side (for balance and looking cool). Rotate hip forward. Strike with the blade of the foot (side) and toes pointed down. Return left foot to side position. Follow-up with another kick or frigg'n book.

Targets: Bellies, neck, and chins

Roundhouse Kick

Start with right side facing target, feet shoulder width apart, and right foot forward. Transfer weight to the right leg. Begin turning towards target, weight on front leg. Lift left knee close to the body. Unload the right knee as turn is executed to avoid knee injury. Rotate right foot, pointing left toe away from kick. Lean slightly to the right at the waist. Point left bended knee at target. Extend left leg outward, but don't hyperextend the knee. Lower right arm to the side (for balance). Rotate left hip forward. Strike with the top of the foot and toes pointed down. Place left foot down wider than shoulder width. You should be facing opposite from start (left side facing target).

Targets: Butt flaps, bikini lines, and lips

You can practice your kicks on trees *or* you can pile a bunch of pillows on top of each other and wrap them in a blanket so they don't fall over.

How to Make Your Own Ninja Suit out of Stuff

Anybody who needs somebody needs a ninja suit. Ninja suits are basically made out of cloth and buttons. Every ninja has one. Most of them are black so they can blend into the night. And if your baby-sitter gives you one because you guys are "homies" but out of nowhere he brings some other kid over who he's been baby-sitting *all along* when you thought you were the only one and you feel cheated and have to rip the suit into chunks because you know that the other kid could never afford one and you want to see him cry, then watch out because baby-sitters only make you feel empty[229] at[230] the[231] end[232] of[233] summer.[234] Anyway, the best place to start for a ninja suit is Gramma. Just tell her you actually want black pajamas this Christmas. But if your gramma is dead from stomach cancer after eating aspirin everyday, you should probably just make your own. Personally, I prefer to make them myself and anyone can, if they have the passion. You just go

---

[229] What did you do that for? I spent forty bucks on that!—**John, ed.**

[230] Why did you bring that other kid over?

[231] I told you—I had to baby-sit you and one of Ms. Evans's boys at the same time.

[232] So what now? Are you best buds with everybody in the neighborhood? Are you some kind of friend slut?

[233] No. But you have some REAL Ultimate Issues.

[234] By issues, you mean Power.

find some black cloth and sew it all together and it should look like this when you're done.

Make Your Own Badass Ninja Weapons

> **Did You Know?**
> Nobody can kill a ninja, so if two ninjas started fighting each other, they would probably malfunction and start beeping and smoking.

In the olden times, ninjas weren't allowed to carry around real weapons. The local governments made having weapons illegal, because they said so. So, basically, they had to make their own to protect themselves from burglars. In this section, I'm going to teach you how to make your own weapons, too.

The difference between dying and *not-dying* might be your perspective. Like, most people, when they look at a pencil, they just see a simple pencil, but a ninja, when *he* looks at the same exact pencil, he sees a super skinny school bus whose wheels popped off. Now, look around your own room for possible weapons. Anything will do. You could knock someone's tooth out with just a simple marble or you can whip their back with a jump rope.

Now, let's get started with making some real weapons.

Ninja Stars

When hanging with their clan, ninjas generally don't toss around real metal ninja stars. 'Cause if one ninja does it, then everybody's going to do it, and then some lamp gets busted and everybody has to go home and then what? They use paper stars that you can make, too. All you need is a sheet[235] of[236] paper[237] and[238] a[239] little[240] bit[241] of[242] anger.[243] Just[244] follow[245] the[246] picture[247] on the right[248] for[249] REAL[250] paper[251] stars.[252]

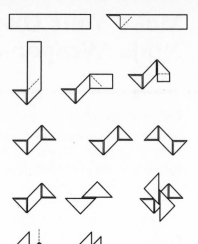

[235] **Hey, come here.**

[236] Yeah, what?

[237] **Is the coast clear?**

[238] What?

[239] **The note, I saw it. I've come to take you away from this place.**

[240] KIDNAP ME?

[241] **Yeah!**

[242] Do you mean it?

[243] **Of course! I got the car running and I made a little bed for you in the living room. There's a refrigerator box for you to play in and everything.**

[244] But what if you stop liking me after a couple days?

[245] **Well, you're going to have to trust me. I'm taking a risk too, you know—you might tear apart my house or rip up the carpet, but I trust that you won't.**

[246] But what if I accidentally rip up the carpet and I really didn't mean it, but, at the time, it looked like I did. Then what?

[247] **Just get in the fucking car!**

[248] What's your problem?

[249] **I'm sorry. I wasn't attacking you. I was only verbalizing my frustration, and I value your opinion. You're just not what I expected, and you surprised me.**

[250] Well, you're not that great either.

[251] **Well, maybe we should just call this whole thing off!**

[252] Maybe we should!

Boner

My ultimate fantasy would be like this: The scene would open up to no smoke. There is a back yard just laying there. The camera moves around and sees this hot babe sitting on a chair, sunbathing. She's very, very hot. Plus, it's summer outside— so she's even hotter. Then the audience will see that she's getting hungry, so she gets a banana from her purse. And just when she opens the banana peel, BOOM! the fence behind her explodes. The camera goes all crazy and jiggles and there's smoke every- where. The babe looks over and sees a gigantic hole in the fence with smoke pouring out. Then music starts pumping up hard. I walk out of the smoky fence-hole real slow, wearing a crotchless gorilla suit. The babe drops the banana and we pork all night long.

Sometimes parents are too busy with themselves to talk to their kids about sex. Maybe this happened to you. Maybe it didn't. I don't know. Or sometimes they're just too shy to talk about pee-pees and wee-wees. So maybe you're the one who has to start the conversation and *teach them*. You can start it from an event you both see—try taking them to the zoo and watch the animals hump. But make sure to use the coolest names for the body parts. This will put them at ease. And make sure you're *approachable*, too. Wear light fitting clothing. Cologne doesn't hurt either. My main point is that if you don't talk to them about sex, your parents may never ask. Teaching a parent about porking can be pretty tough, but you can begin with one of the hottest topics alive—the boner. Ninjas have the best ones and everybody else's is just "not bad." And don't worry if yours isn't normal. There isn't really any normal. If yours looks different than the other kids in gym class, that's O.K. And if yours isn't as big as theirs either, that's O.K., too! You probably have special talents they don't have. Maybe you can climb the rope faster than every- body else or you're super smart. But if you're not the smartest or tallest, maybe you can do the splits in the bathtub and there isn't anybody else who can do that. So they can shut their mouth.

The ninja would never pork somebody who would just use them for their own personal benefit or who would say they like you thiiiiiiiiiiiiiiiiiiiiiiiiiiiiiiiiiiiiis much, but only like you thiiis much. And if you want to be a real ninja, you should only mate with someone who likes you for YOU, not because you can slam dunk or smoke or have a driver's license—that's ludicrous. If you have trouble getting started, here are some qualities you should probably look for in a mate:

- Has to be good at video games (maybe not all of them, but a good amount)
- Doesn't care if room is messy, 'cause it really doesn't matter in the end
- Living in an aquatic city has to be a possibility, but she can't be obsessed with it—that might be a turnoff
- Good at cards, but not too good
- Nice
- Friendly
- Doesn't have a beard, but if she does, then it has to be temporary
- Likes chili
- Good at kites
- Knowledge about robots and time travel is a plus, but isn't a necessity
- Likes dogs (will let them French face or ears)
- Won't yell at you
- Doesn't have club feet, but if she does, has to be able to hit a baseball with them
- Doesn't get drunk, puke, and make you clean it up with *your* beach towel

- Won't slap you in the mouth
- Will be your mate till one[253] of[254] you[255] dies[256]
- That's[257] it![258]

A Ninja Makes a Telephone Call

Guy: Hello

Ninja: Hey.

Guy: What do you want?

Ninja: Just called to see if you enjoyed getting your ass beat?

Guy: Wouldn't know.

Ninja: Yeah, right. I beat your ass so bad, you must have forgot.

Guy: Maybe, I beat YOUR ASS so bad YOU forgot!

Ninja: The only thing I forgot was how stupid you are, but you just reminded me. Thanks.

Guy: What kind of person gets their ass beat and then turns around and thinks they beat somebody's ass?

Ninja: You.

---

[253] Dad, do you know where Francine's at? I can't find her anywhere.

[254] She ran away.

[255] How do you know, *Dad*?

[256] Well, I'd run away too if I had to hang out with a retard everyday.

[257] She wouldn't do that!

[258] Well, she's gone. Get used to it.

Ninja Sword

The scene opens up to about a billion pirates laughing their asses off. *What could they be laughing at,* the audience will probably ask. All the pirates look SOOO confident. The audience will then see the back of a ninja, facing all the pirates. His uniform is pure black. He's alone and he doesn't even blink, but the pirates do and when they start thinking about blinking and their eyes being dry, they can't stop. Then one pirate runs over and hands the ninja a note. He opens it up and it says, "There's no way you're going to beat the pirates. You're just one retarded ninja and there are so many of us and we're awesome." The ninja calmly folds up the piece of paper and places it in his front pocket. Then he takes out a pen and writes them a letter that says, "Yeah, right." He folds it hard and throws it at the messenger's face and it cuts his forehead. Then the pirates take turns reading it and they get so mad. Finally, one pirate rips it up, because he's so full of anger. All the pirates start running to kill the ninja. As they run toward this lonely simple ninja, pump-up music starts playing slowly. Everybody is running at him real slow. The ninja pulls out his sword and his hand grips it so hard that blood drips from his knuckles, and when the blood hits the ground, grass starts exploding in slow-mo. Then the ninja digs his feet into the ground and the pirates get their toys ready. And, as they're about to get the ninja, BOOM! the ninja swings his sword so hard, a nuclear explosion happens right on one guy's frigg'n face and pump-up music comes harder than it was playing earlier and the ninja grows about a thousand feet tall and his suit grows, too, and the pirates' butts pucker because of fear and the ninja's voice sounds like an angry monster and WHAM! he would just frigg'n stomp on the frigg'n wimps and they would explode so hard. And the ninja chases them down a hill where they start slipping because it rained earlier and the ninja starts cutting down mountains and mountains start screaming and he sees the last bunch of pirates crumpled up in a pasture, squealing, and the ninja bends over and starts munching on them like a crazy cow. And then the ninja slams his sword in the ground and flies off into space because no one understands him and the sword is still there somewhere in that silly pasture where a bunch of animals sniff it and don't even understand what the hell happened on that badass Sunday.

Now, I bet you can't stop thinking about ninja swords. I will never stop thinking about them. The best way to express your feelings about somebody you don't like is to cut off their head. That way, there's no misunderstanding. Oh, hello, didn't you say that I'm the only kid you'll ever baby-sit? Oh, you don't go around town and baby-sit anybody with two legs? Then BOOM! That neck is spitting sap all over the front lawn. And, oh, you want to be buddies till we die? That sounds really nice. Oh, wait, you changed your mind? I understand. And then I start punching you until my hand breaks through your chest and I rip up all the cords. And oh, we're not having spicy chili tonight? Nobody cares what I want for dinner? Then how about I stomp on your face till it looks like spicy chili and then I'll eat it in a fancy restaurant full of people just begging to hang out with me.

Ninjas don't mess around and lie to you like certain people do. Ninjas kill people. And even if they kill you, at least you know how they really feel about you. And isn't that worth dying for? I mean, everybody has to die of something. Everybody. And I don't know about you, but it would be a lot sweeter if my gravestone said, "A sweet ass ninja killed this badass kid," than if it said, "This moron choked on a plum." So if you have any brains, you should probably pick the first one. But that's just my personal opinion.

Now, if you can't find a sword laying around your house, you can probably use something else. The bad part is that you have to hit somebody A LOT to kill them with a fake sword, but sometimes that isn't a problem. To make a fake sword, you can either cut one out of cardboard or just use some plastic knives. I would prefer to use cardboard because you can make a much huger sword, but sometimes you just want to have small[259] ones[260] so[261] you[262] can[263] fit[264] them[265] in[266] your[267] backpack.[268]

---

[259] John.

[260] Yeah.

[261] Take this.

[262] This is your book. What do you want me to do with it?

[263] I'm leaving and somebody has to spread the word about ninjas and most, importantly, REAL Ultimate Power. Plus, I'm done with everybody's crap, even yours.

[264] I'm not the enemy, man. I was just trying to help you out. Everyone was in their own way, I guess. What about your parents? Don't you think they'll worry?

[265] Look, amigo, sometimes there comes somebody, maybe once every couple thousand years, who is just too sweet for parents. I have a feeling that person is me.

[266] So this is it, huh? Do you need a ride?

[267] I don't need a ride to where I'm going.

[268] Alright, whatever.

When Ninjas Die

Before a ninja leaves his house, he's got to be fearless. There's so much to be afraid of: bats, monsters, clowns, kidnappers, and floating eyes. But everybody's afraid of dying, which is weird because death happens to everyone. It would be like being afraid of peeing in the shower—it's gonna happen, so why get all crazy about it?

I used to be really scared about dying when I was younger. But, listen homey, there isn't much to worry about. I mean, think about when you were in your mother's vagina, before you were born. Everything was fluffy and warm. Nobody was yelling at you; and if they were, it was muffled and funny sounding. And I bet you were pretty cranky and afraid when you had to come out. But now, if I were to ask if you wanted to go back, you'd say, "No way! That would be sick." Well, that's kinda what heaven's like—you're afraid to go, but once you get there you don't want to come back to Earth, because it would be like sticking your head back into your mom's vagina. So when you look at it that way, there's really not much for you to be afraid of, since you'll enjoy heaven in the end. And guess what, in heaven, parents are a faux pas. And ninjas and kids can hang out whenever they like. And in heaven, you use your mind to do things instead of your body. You can just leave your body on Earth for animals to chew on. There are no physical or mental boundaries either—you can even smoke a breadstick, if you have the willpower. And there are bubbles and clouds and floating pillows that play soft music. And if you're worried that ninjas can't kill people in heaven, you can relax and have another sip of pop. Just because they're in heaven doesn't mean they are any less sweet. The game is the same, but the rules are just a little different. Instead of using ropes and pajama pants to strangle people, they use clouds and halos, which really isn't that bad when you think about it. Other than verything's pretty much the same. I hope you feel better cause I know I do. See ya later, amigo!

How to Commit Seppuku with a Frisbee

Seppuku is the ancient art of killing yourself if you get super pissed and can't find anybody else to kill. Ninjas use all sorts of crap to kill themselves—guns, ropes, knives, lasers, spears, etc.—and don't even think twice about it. These guys would kill themselves for just about any reason and often for no reason at all. That's why there are so few ninjas today.

But if you want to commit seppuku and you're like me, you don't have access to stuff like lasers. But there's hope. I tried to commit seppuku by swallowing a Frisbee a couple of times—and believe me, it's pretty cool. The only catch is you have to be *really* super pissed off to do it.

Step 1:   Get a frisbee from the store or a friend.

Step 2:   Clean the Frisbee.

Step 3:   Make sure your parents aren't around.

Step 4:   Put something slippery on it, like butter or cream.

Step 5:   Get *really*, super pissed.

Step 6:   Fold the Frisbee, hard (this is crucial).

Step 7:   Keep folded and insert Frisbee into mouth, hard.

Step 8:   Push hard until you can't see it.

Step 9:   Wait.

Step 10: Die.

Step 5

Step 6

Step 8

If you succeed, everybody will be like, "Holy crap!" But if you don't succeed, try again tomorrow, but do it even **harder**.

Little Tiny Hippo (continued)

SCENE 2:
After a bunch of ninjas finish completely beating the pirates'
butts, the ninjas go searching for the little tiny hippo. They find
Roberq hiding in bushes/leaves and he's completely freaking out.
One ninja nicely leans over and says, "Yo, do wanna hang out
with us?" And the little tiny hippo asks, "Like best friends and
everything?" And the ninjas are like, "Totally, and that's a fact."

Then Roberq's new best friends take him to a super safe place
hidden deep inside a huge magical forest full of sweetness
where no little hippos are insulted or beaten
and hippos can be whatever they want
and most importantly
where someone
would listen
to
me.

$\mathcal{F}in$(ished)

Appendix and Exhibits

Once there was this bird who lived with a bunch of other birds who treated him like crap. But then, one day, the bird found an egg roll laying on a snowy hill and took it back to the base. Everybody was like, "Gimme some." And the bird was like, "Remember when you said all that crap about me?" And the other birds got real quiet. "Well, I do." And the bird laid a log right on the floor.

—Ancient Chinese Proverb

BRINGING EVERYTHING TOGETHER: THE OFFICIAL NINJA GAME

The Official Ninja Game is a chance to bring together everything that you've learned from the book and have some great fun with your buddies.

Rules:

The winner is the ninja that accumulates the most N-points (ninja points) in a specified amount of time. The preferable time frame is one day to one week.

Points are achieved by performing activities that are honorable, sweet, or crazy, according to the standards set by *REAL Ultimate Power: The Official Ninja Book*. An honorable act is honorable according to The Ninja Code of Honor. For example, peeing on a friend's back is honorable. A sweet act is an act that is just plain sweet. For example, doing a naked back flip into a lake is pretty sweet. A crazy act is an act that is pretty nuts. For example, giving a speech while doing the splits the entire time is pretty absurd (unless you're doing a speech on the splits—then it's just natural).

Each activity must be seen by at least one homey.

The point value is rated on the Flipometer™, where a point value of "1" is a **neat** honorable, sweet, or crazy act. And a point value of "10" is a **totally sweet** honorable, sweet, or crazy act. (So it's possible to perform a totally sweet, sweet act.)

After all the points have been totaled for the specified time period, the player with the most N-points wins.

Note, each player is on the honest system. Lying about doing something cool is not cool.

N-Card (Ninja Card)			
Name:	Honorable Acts Description	Sweet Stuff Description	Crazy Things Description
Activity Name:	☐ Pt. value	☐ Pt. value	☐ Pt. value
Activity Name:	☐ Pt. value	☐ Pt. value	☐ Pt. value
Activity Name:	☐ Pt. value	☐ Pt. value	☐ Pt. value

EXHIBIT A:
HISTORY PAPER ON RITALIN

Benjamin Franklin
by Robert Hamburger

Benjamin Franklin is good. He helped make the Declaration of Independence AND invented electricity. He was born in Boston in 1707. He was always questing to be perfect. He invented the slogan "practice makes perfect." We should all try to be perfect everyday. But, eventually, Benjamin Franklin never became perfect. And there was a revolution, not because of him, though. Many people died in the war, except Benjamin Franklin. He lived in Boston.

On April 17, 1790, Benjamin Franklin finally died. Over 20,000 people attended his funeral. But his life is best summed up by the epitaph on his gravestone "Goodbye everyone, till we meet again in heaven with our dad, Jesus Christ."

A -

Excellent rough draft! I can't wait to see the final copy. I would like to talk to your parents and tell them how good this is, and how well you've been behaving! Great Work! I am truly impressed by your improvement Love. Ms. Burbell

EXHIBIT B:
HISTORY PAPER OFF RITALIN

Benjamin Franklin

by Robert Hamburger

Benjamin Franklin killed somebody once. And he porked a turtle, too—a big one. Let me explain.

August 2, 6:19 P.M. Benjamin Franklin left his home to meet Joseph Quimby, a typesetter whom Franklin befriended twenty-one hours prior. It was not uncommon those days for two people to develop a friendship for the stupidest reasons. And Mr. Quimby and Mr. Franklin did just that. They had first met at a roller rink. Both men wore a size ten-and-a-half skate and there was only one pair of size ten-and-a-half skates left at the rink. This produced scuffling. But Franklin had an idea. He had Mr. Quimby stand next to him, side by side, and they fastened their belts together. Now, with Franklin on the left side and Quimby on the right, Franklin put on the left skate, while Quimby put on the right. And together, for at least fifteen minutes, they locked arms and skated as one. Several people gasped, but got over it. And afterward, they decided to be friends and exchanged numbers. But that's neither here nor there. What's important is that in one hour, Quimby would be dead and Franklin would be inside another species.

August 2, 6:49 P.M. Franklin arrived at the Quimby residence. It was warm outside, but not too warm.

August 2, 6:50 P.M. Quimby answered the door. They began fighting.

August 2, 6:52 P.M. The two stopped fighting and Quimby invited Franklin inside for coffee. According the maid, Katherine O'Foley, the pair sat in the study and looked out the window for five minutes. They were friends now and everybody knew it.

August 2, 7:02 P.M. After some chitchat, Franklin confronted Quimby about thinking he was too cool to hang out with him. According to the maid, Quimby denied the accusation and tried to explain why he didn't hang out earlier that afternoon. But when Franklin began screaming, Ms. O'Foley ran from the house to find help. What happened thereafter is pure speculation.

August 2, approximately 7:15 P.M. Evidence from the scene suggests that Quimby ran behind his desk and hid underneath. Franklin then turned over the desk and dragged Quimby toward the center of the room. There, Franklin scratched up the victim's face with his claws and bit his chest open.

August 2, approximately 7:20 P.M. As the victim's body lay face up, Franklin unzipped his tights and urinated on it, repeating, "We destroy to rebuild—and through this process comes perfection. But, in the end, we discover perfection is also empty, just as a friendship founded on roller skates." Before finishing, Franklin noticed a hairless green head peering through the window, fogging up the pane with panic. This little head was attached to a Galapagos turtle,[269] who had *seen everything*. Mr. Franklin scurried to the window. Determined to escape, the turtle tried desperately to walk away, but the old man was pissed. Franklin grabbed the turtle and slapped him on Quimby's chest. Instinctively, the animal retracted all its limbs inside the impenetrable shell.

---

[269] Galapagos turtles are members of the reptilian family. These animals are found on the Galapagos Islands and at zoos for people to look at. They are best known for their size and age. They can get up to two-hundred-years-old! (Encyclopedia Britannica, Volume G, p. 57.)

August 2, approximately 7:24 P.M. After having little success cracking it open, Benjamin Franklin had the idea to get the turtle to peak his head out the shell. So, once again, he unzipped his tights and, with his chicken-colored chest exposed, he lay with the turtle in feigned passion. Appalled, the turtle popped his head out to reprimand the assailant. But just then, Franklin grabbed the head with his thumb and forefinger and, with a light tug, detached it from the body and popped it in his mouth like a peanut.

Benjamin Franklin died on April 17, 1790. Over 20,000 people attended his funeral. But his life is best summed up by the epitaph on his grave-stone: "Yo, I invented electricity—so get out of my face."

F

I would like to talk to your parents and ask them what they feed you.

Mr. Burbell

Exhibit C:
Popular Girl's Note

Sally,

Here's the hot scoop. Tanya likes Billy, but Billy doesn't know. Tanya thinks Billy likes Maria. But everybody thinks that just 'cause he sits next to Maria during math, but Billy just does that so he can copy her homework. O.K.? Now I heard from Michelle that Tanya would dry ride anybody. I think it's true—you should see how she eats a lollipop. So we can't let her find out that Billy doesn't really like Maria! Now, if someone would just tell Tanya that *Mike* likes her and that he would like to dry ride "sometime" then maybe she would leave Billy alone. I'm just saying that it might be a good idea, 'cause I heard from somebody that I like Billy and it might be true. But who knows for sure? Oh, and by the way, you know *Robert-the-freak*? He is so weird! Yesterday, he ate eight bowls of spicy chili during lunch and he's the one who puked on the stairs. And now Ms. Cray will be in the hospital till Thursday, which sucks because she's so cool!

Peace!
Cathy

EXHIBIT D:
A ONE HUNDRED–WORD ESSAY

Kicking
by Robert Hamburger

Kicking people is bad. Many people get seriously hurt from kicking each year and they should not have to live with that. Nobody should. And when some people can't control themselves, stuff like that happens. People like me, who can't control themselves, have to realize that other people have dreams and fantasies they can't pursue if they get kicked. Other people deserve better. Therefore, kicking is bad and people shouldn't ever do it, because it's wrong and it ruins the lives of everyone involved. I promise I will never do it again. And I apologize to Margaret and her family.

EXHIBIT E: IRS LETTER TO MR. AND MRS. HAMBURGER

Mr. and Mrs. Hamburger,

This letter is in reply to your queries regarding your son, Robert Hamburger. You are correct that to claim Robert as a dependent in your 1040 tax form, you are required to provide the necessities of living—food, shelter, clothing— and that under IRS publication 17, Chapter 3, you needn't afford Robert toys or take him to the zoo or be emotionally available. Such activities are beyond the scope of personal exemptions for dependents.

Furthermore, it also isn't necessary for you to keep the same last name as Robert. You are free to change your last name if you feel embarrassed of his behavior. You only need to contact the IRS regarding such a change so that your forms are processed properly for next year's return (form 8822, line 5).

Lastly, I am not familiar enough with children to make any legitimate diagnosis of your son's problem. Though, my sister's boy was obsessed with ponies a couple years ago. But after his parents told him that only girls like ponies and consistently humiliated him in front of family and friends, he gave in and started hating ponies. You might want to try something like that. It was quite effective in my nephew's case.

Thanks,
Cindy Ordonez
Internal Revenue Service

NINJA MAP

Lava pit

This where the lava snakes and lava monkeys are. Most people don't know that, but it's nothing to really worry about because as long as you run through this part, you'll be fine.

Ms. Evan's house

She never cuts her lawn, because of laziness. So the grass is long. This is a good spot for ninjas to hide and throw stuff into the street.

Graveyard

This is where the graveyard is at. It's not a real graveyard though, because nobody died there, but this kid Mike fell asleep here and nobody could find him for a couple hours. And now it's full of ghosts.

Crazy People Live Here

These people are crazy. They tried selling their house a while ago and they were talking to this lady and they were like, "Do you want it?" And the lady was like, "No," because the walls were carpeted and there was chicken blood all over the place.

Ninja Lookout

This is were ninjas can see who's coming in and out of the neighborhood. It doesn't belong to anybody, but there's a box of porno magazines up in that tree.

Ninja Hideout

This is where a ninja clan lives. Mark said he saw a few sleeping there one night, but it was really late. He said that he was freaking out when he saw them laying there, under grass blankets. Dad said he hit a ninja late at night, and he had me go outside to show me the dent on his car, and he said that it proved ninjas were vulnerable and boring. He's a liar.

Bathroom

Ninjas go to the bathroom here. Sometimes it's in large clumps and other times it's in small pellets.

GLOSSARY

Baby-sitter: Someone who your mom pays to play with you. They're fun to hang out with, but they just leave you feeling empty at the end of the summer.

Boner: When you look at Mom's magazines and can't look away.

Child psychiatrist: Asshole.

Diaper: Basically, they're pants for babies and artists.

Dogs: What a mom should be, minus the fur.

Emotions/Sensitivity: Something little diaper babies have.

Expressing yourself: Something you do if you can't get a real job.

Father: An adult male that produces offspring for spanking purposes.

Frenching: Putting your tongue all the way inside someone's ear and leaving it there for over three seconds.

Friendship: Something that should last forever, but some people are idiots.

Hippos: The most underrated mammal to ever exist. Most people don't like them because they don't know them or they're just jealous.

Japan: Asian country, island.

Ki: An energy that happens when you think about the last time you were spanked. You can focus that energy into power.

Karate: A fighting style that ninjas scoff at because it's strictly for retards.

Kitana: Ninja weapon.

Mother: Similar to a father, but owns a vagina.

Ninja: A deadly assassin who has the power to do whatever he wants no matter what.

Numchucks: Ninja weapon.

Pork: When you pork a hot babe.

Puberty: Leaving your friends behind.

Pubic hair: Foreshadowing.

Sai: Ninja weapon.

Seat belt: A life saving device in cars. My friend Mark's dad says that we should always wear our seat belts. He worked as a car repair man for fifteen years and, believe me, he's picked out enough hair from broken windshields to know what he's talking about.

Sensei: Teaches the ninja how to be a ninja.

Slam dunk: When somebody jumps up and slams the ball right into the basket.

Sleep-over: When one buddy likes another buddy more than a classmate, but less than a husband, he'll propose to have the buddy sleep over for pizza and pop.

Sperm: White pee.

Throw up: What you have to clean up with *your towel* when Mom takes too many pills.

Treason: Saying you're gonna hang out, but never showing up.

Vagina: Where babies pop out and boners pop in.

Women: Vomitable, except the hot ones.

Ying and yang: Ying represents total sweetness, hanging out, relaxing, and just plain coolness. And the Yang represents people who can't shut their mouth. The two fight against each other non-stop. An imbalance in your Ying Yang can cause illnesses like mumps, measles, or even chicken pox.

Zen: Most people believe that Zen is becoming one with a hot babe or with yourself when your parents aren't home. Others believe Zen is like Nirvana, but without the sleeping bags—if you know what I mean. I don't know what to believe. I guess it's just a really nice place.

QUIZ

Since you finished reading my book about ninjas, you can now test your ninja knowledge. But, if you didn't read the book yet, you can test yourself to see if you need to. And if you only read half, you can see if need to read the other half. After taking the test, you can also see what belt you are. Good luck, amigos!

1. **Which is the sweetest?**
   A. Samurais
   B. Ninjas
   C. Aliens
   D. Pirates

2. **What would a ninja want to do most?**
   A. Eat a bowl of soup out of an exploded skull
   B. Strangle somebody with pajama pants
   C. Kill somebody right when they get off death row after being proven innocent
   D. Bite somebody's finger just as they bite into a hot dog, applying the same amount of pressure as victim uses on the hot dog

3. **Where do most ninjas hang out?**
   A. Friend's house
   B. Forest
   C. Dojos
   D. City

4. **What is a ninja's favorite meal?**
   A. Breakfast
   B. Lunch
   C. Beating somebody's ass HARD, because they can't shut their mouth
   D. Dinner

5. **How do ninjas eat?**

    A. With their hands
    B. With someone else's hand
    C. With pizzazz
    D. With a buddy

6. **If someone bumps into a ninja on the street, a ninja will probably**

    A. Say he's sorry, because it's not worth getting into a big fight over such a silly thing.
    B. Smile and excuse himself, because it might have been his fault—who knows?
    C. Use this as a chance to introduce himself, because we're all in this together and any opportunity to exchange human warmth is truly worthwhile in such a cruel and lonely world.
    D. Fill the guy's mouth full of ninja stars, because he probably bumps into people all day and laughs about it at home cause he's a frigg'n asshole.

7. **Which epitaph is a real ninja epitaph? (Epitaphs are the things written on grave stones.)**

    A. Yo, whoever did this is frigg'n dead.
    B. THIS IS BULLCRAP!
    C. I'd like to give a shout out to my homeboys, Tyrone, Jesse, Ice-Caream, Shauntell, and Crazy Nutz. PEACE.
    D. I came. I saw. I crapped my pants.

8. **A ninja is playing at a friend's house when the friend goes to the bathroom and leaves the ninja alone with a room full of toys. Does the ninja . . .**

    A. Continue to play quietly till the buddy comes back and doesn't ask any questions about their poop?
    B. Go bang on the bathroom door, screaming for them to hurry up, 'cause sometimes a bunch of toys doesn't make the emptiness go away?

    C. Just leave, 'cause his buddy should have waited to go till they were completely finished playing 'cause that's what people do?

    D. Sprinkle pubes on his pillow case?

9. What does a ninja do if he's playing a board game with someone and he starts losing the game?

    A. Calmly flip the game over so the pieces spray everywhere and start saying what a bunch of bullcrap the whole thing is

    B. Politely excuse himself to take a dump and then escape through the bathroom window so he never actually loses the game

    C. Start kicking his feet *nonstop* and screaming

    D. Spit up all over his chest

10. What would a ninja do if somebody asked him what time it was?

    A. Peacefully look at his watch and say the time nicely and calmly

    B. Pretend that he didn't hear the guy, but if he asks again, the ninja would start running

    C. Smile and start talking about the history of clocks and bedtimes and stuff

    D. Pull up his sleeve, revealing his badass watch and when the guy bends over to look, the ninja would snap his wrist upward and crumple the guy's nose, and then run

11. What is the most precious quality a ninja wants in a friend?

    A. Be there to get a mom for help when his kneecap pops off

    B. Always tell the truth, even if it hurts, but at least he'll know

    C. Listen to him, or at least pretend to, and then ask follow-up questions

    D. Be a hippo

12. **What would a ninja do with a hot babe?**
    A. Stay up all night with her and make a list of all the qualities she would want in a future husband
    B. Cut out pictures in magazines of dream houses with her and make a huge collage
    C. Become vulnerable to her by revealing his deepest darkest secrets and *actively* listening to her and connecting with her emotionally *and spiritually*
    D. Pork

Now, every correct answer counts for one point, even the hard ones. Add your score together to figure out what belt you are!

Correct Answers   1. B, 2. D, 3. C, 4. B, 5. D, 6. D, 7. B, 8. D, 9. A, 10. D, 11. D, 12. D.

The Nine Belts of Power

Score 0–1
White Belt   Diaper Baby   You're just starting out—so what did you expect? Get a life or go back to bed.

Score 2–3
Yellow Belt   Butthole   Self-explanatory.

Score 4–5
Green Belt   Idiot   You're probably just like everybody else. Boring and scared.

Score 6–7
Orange Belt   Moron   Either you're hopeless or you just need to concentrate.

Score 8–9
Blue Belt   Guy   You're alright.

Score 10–11
Purple Belt   Dude   You're almost there. Maybe
                              you're not pumped up
                              enough . . .

Score 12
Black Belt   Ninja   You have REAL Ultimate Power.
                              Don't let anybody ever tell you
                              that you're not good enough,
                              cause you're a ninja and nobody
                              can take that away.[270]

------

[270] If you didn't do that well on the test, you can still be a ninja. So don't get too
worried.

DISCLAIMER

Good evening. Killing people, individually or a bunch at a time, is an art—a very cool art. You should only do it if you are completely sure you are totally sweet. (Many people think they're pretty cool, but they're not. I'm sure you know someone like this—maybe a friend or a relative. You just need to keep away from these people—they don't know anything. There was this one kid, you probably don't know him, but he thought he was so frigg'n sweet, and you know what? He wasn't.) So if you *don't* have what it takes—I mean, REAL Ultimate Power—you probably need to chill. No joke.

271, 272, 273, 274, 275

---

271 Francine.

272 Yes, Robert.

273 Where are we?

274 I don't know. Are you pumped?

275 Are you kidding? I'm ALWAYS pumped.

ABOUT THE AUTHOR

Robert Hamburger has a black belt in Street Fighter 2, and a second degree black belt in Mortal Kombat 1–3. He can kick or punch the wall without feeling pain. He has studied ninjas for several weeks and has watched a ton of movies about them. Robert lives with a bunch of hot babes and porks them *whenever he wants*. This is his first book.

ABOUT THE ARTIST

James Novy is awesome at drawing. He has lived next door to Robert for a couple years. When he heard that Robert was going to make a book about ninjas James wanted to help out real bad. His favorite things are baseball, surfing, martial arts, and ninjas.